CW01394735

Everyday Classics: Fourth Reader

Ashley Horace Thorndike, Franklin Thomas Baker

Nabu Public Domain Reprints:

You are holding a reproduction of an original work published before 1923 that is in the public domain in the United States of America, and possibly other countries. You may freely copy and distribute this work as no entity (individual or corporate) has a copyright on the body of the work. This book may contain prior copyright references, and library stamps (as most of these works were scanned from library copies). These have been scanned and retained as part of the historical artifact.

This book may have occasional imperfections such as missing or blurred pages, poor pictures, errant marks, etc. that were either part of the original artifact, or were introduced by the scanning process. We believe this work is culturally important, and despite the imperfections, have elected to bring it back into print as part of our continuing commitment to the preservation of printed works worldwide. We appreciate your understanding of the imperfections in the preservation process, and hope you enjoy this valuable book.

"Through books we may, without stirring from our firesides, roam to the remotest regions of the earth."

— Edwin P. Whipple.

He Came, and Wrestled with Mondamin.

EVERYDAY CLASSICS

FOURTH READER

BY

FRANKLIN T. BAKER

PROFESSOR OF ENGLISH IN TEACHERS COLLEGE
AND SUPERVISOR OF ENGLISH IN THE
HORACE MANN SCHOOL

AND

ASHLEY H. THORNDIKE

PROFESSOR OF ENGLISH IN COLUMBIA UNIVERSITY

ILLUSTRATED BY WILLY POGANY

New York
THE MACMILLAN COMPANY
1918

All rights reserved

Educt 759.18,190

HARVARD COLLEGE LIBRARY
GIFT OF
ALBERT BUSHNELL HART

DEC 5 1923

COPYRIGHT, 1917,

BY THE MACMILLAN COMPANY.

Set up and electrotyped. Published February, 1917.
Reprinted June, 1917. September, 1917.

PREFACE

The EVERYDAY CLASSICS is a series of school readers based upon a valid principle and a vital need. The principle is that there is a considerable body of good literature, known to all people who know books, and simple enough to be understood and enjoyed by children. Much of it, indeed, is of most value if read in childhood, and retained through life as a permanent influence upon one's attitude towards life. The need of such a series is seen in the fact that many children are not put in touch with much of this common heritage of the race. In the teacher's natural desire to find something new and different, many of the old and approved things have been pushed aside.

A classic is something more easily known than defined. It is not necessarily abstruse, difficult, or remote from common life. It is a piece of literature that has received the approval of good judges for a long enough time to make that approval settled. Like good music, it cannot grow old; it is last year's rag-time that becomes unpleasant, not the good old songs. A classic may be as old as Homer, or as new as Hawthorne; it may be as difficult as Dante, or as simple as Mother Goose. Indeed, a large proportion of the classics of the world are very

5

simple. In Æsop, and Homer, and the old fairy tales, and many of the great stories of the world, like *Robinson Crusoe,* simplicity is one of the highest merits.

This series, by its very purpose, rejects " new " material. There is a place for that, but not in the plan of this series. We have therefore chosen what is common, established, almost proverbial; what has become indisputably " classic "; what, in brief, every child in the land ought to know, because it is good and because other people know it. And it is well to remember that what is old to us is new to the child. The little pigs that went to market, Little Red Riding Hood, Gulliver and Sindbad are to him fresh creations of the imagination which open the door of an enchanted world.

The educational worth of such material calls for no defense. In an age when the need of socializing and unifying our people is keenly felt, the value of a common stock of knowledge, a common set of ideals, is obvious. A people is best unified by being taught in childhood the best things in its intellectual and moral heritage. Our own heritage is, like our ancestry, composite. Hebrew, Greek, Roman, English, French, and Teutonic elements are blended in our cultural past. We draw from these and retain what suits our composite racial and national spirit. An introduction to the best of this common heritage is one of our ways of making good citizens. Not what we *know* only, but what we have *felt* and *enjoyed*, largely determines what we are.

The FOURTH READER of this series is made up of fanciful tales of adventure, stories about real heroes, descriptions of out-of-door life, stories about children and their adventures, and patriotic selections. It includes also poetry of a simple type, most of it selected for its treatment of nature.

The editors have supplied brief lists of words that may be difficult or that need to be noted carefully, and added to them occasionally a definition and usually a phonetic key to the pronunciation. Most of the teaching of the words, however, must be done, as needed, on the teacher's own initiative. A further feature of the book is the short list of simple questions to enable the child to see for himself whether he has really understood the story. Of late years there is an increasing interest in these "reading tests"; we realize that even when the child reads the words aloud correctly, it is by no means certain that he has got the meaning of the selection.

There have been added, also, certain questions leading to further simple activities, as oral or written composition and dramatization. In these and other ways the editors have sought to bring the reading close to the interests and lives of the children.

CONTENTS

IMAGINARY TRAVELS

NATURE AND OUT-OF-DOORS

PATRIOTIC SELECTIONS

HISTORICAL TALES AND LEGENDS

STORIES OF CHILD LIFE

STORIES AND POEMS

THE MILLER AND THE KING.

A SONG OF THE SEA

A wet sheet and a flowing sea,
And a wind that follows fast
And fills the white and rustling sail
And bends the gallant mast;
And bends the gallant mast, my boys,   5
While, like the eagle free,
Away the good ship flies, and leaves
Old England on our lee.

O for a soft and gentle wind!
I heard a fair one cry;
But give to me the swelling breeze,
And white waves heaving high;
5 The white waves heaving high, my lads,
The good ship tight and free —
The world of waters is our home,
And merry men are we.

There's tempest in yon hornéd moon,
10 And lightning in yon cloud;
But hark the music, mariners!
The wind is piping loud;
The wind is piping loud, my boys,
The lightning flashes free —
15 While the hollow oak our palace is,
Our heritage the sea.

ALLAN CUNNINGHAM.

heritage (hĕr'it ăj) : that which one inherits, or comes into by right of birth

hollow oak : ships used to be built of wood

lee (lē) : the sheltered side

sheet (shēt) : in sailors' language, the rope that ties the lower part of the sail to the boat

yon : yonder, that

GULLIVER IN LILLIPUT

There have been many stories invented, that is, made up, about make-believe places. One of the best known of these is *Gulliver's Travels*, by Jonathan Swift, who lived in Dublin two hundred years ago. He has his imaginary traveler, Gulliver, go first to Lilliput, where the people are about six inches high. Everything else in Lilliput is on the same scale. Then Gulliver goes to Brobdingnag, where the people are sixty feet high. There again everything is on the same scale of great size. You will enjoy reading the rest of the book, and seeing how clever the author is in carrying out his ideas.

I

On the fifth of November, which was the beginning of summer in the South Sea, we spied a rock within half a cable's length of the ship; but the wind was so strong that we were driven directly upon it, and immediately wrecked. Six of the 5 crew, of whom I was one, having let down the boat into the sea, succeeded in getting clear of the ship and rock.

We trusted ourselves to the mercy of the waves, and in about half an hour the boat was overturned 10

by a sudden gust from the north. What became
of my companions in the boat, as well as those
who escaped on the rock, I could not tell, but I
concluded that they were all lost.

5 For my own part, I swam as fortune directed
me, and was pushed forward by wind and tide.
I was almost exhausted, when I suddenly found
myself in shallow water; and by this time the
storm had gone down. I walked nearly a mile
10 before I got to the shore, and from there went
nearly half a mile across the country, but could
not discover any sign of houses or inhabitants.

I was extremely tired, and with that, and the
heat of the weather, I found myself very sleepy.
15 I lay down on the grass, which was very short
and soft, where I slept more soundly than ever
I remember to have done in my life. When
I waked, it was just daylight. I attempted to
rise, but was not able to stir; for as I happened
20 to lie on my back, I found my arms and legs were
strongly fastened on each side to the ground, and
my hair, which was long and thick, was tied down
in the same manner. I heard a confused noise

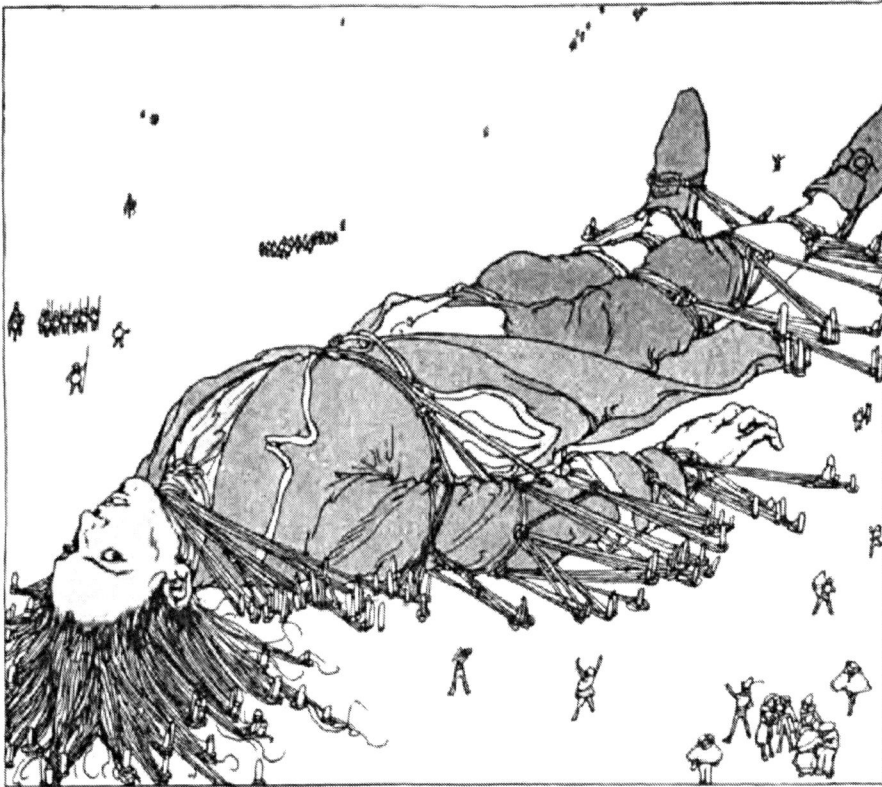

about me, but, in the position I lay, could see nothing but the sky.

In a little while I felt something alive moving on my left leg, and moving gently forward on my breast until it came almost up to my chin; then turning my eyes downward as much as I could, I perceived it to be a human creature not six inches high, with a bow and arrow in his hands, and a quiver at his back. In the meantime, I felt at least forty more of the same kind following the first. I was in the utmost astonishment, and roared so loudly, that they all ran back in a 5 fright; and some of them, as I was afterward told, were hurt with the falls they got by leaping from my sides upon the ground. They soon returned, however, and one of them, who ventured so far as to get a full sight of my face, lifting up 10 his hands and eyes in wonder, said a few words in a shrill voice. The others repeated these words several times, but I knew not what they meant.

I lay all this while, in great uneasiness; at 15 length, struggling to get loose, I had the luck to break the strings, and wrench out the pegs that fastened my left arm to the ground. At the same time, with a violent pull which gave me very great pain, I loosened the strings that tied 20 down my hair on the left side, so that I was able to turn my head about two inches. But the creatures ran off a second time, before I could seize them; whereupon there was a great shout in a very shrill accent, and in an instant I felt a hundred arrows shot into my left hand, which pricked me like so many needles.

When this shower of arrows was over, I tried again to get loose, but they sent another vol-5 ley larger than the first, and some of them attempted with spears to stick me in the sides. By good luck I had on a buff jerkin, which they could not pierce. I thought it the most prudent method to lie still, and when the people saw 10 that I was quiet, they discharged no more arrows. But by the noise I heard, I knew their numbers increased; and about four yards from me, near my right ear, I heard a knocking for more than an hour, like that of people at work. On turn-15 ing my head that way, as well as the pegs and strings would permit me, I saw a stage built about a foot and a half from the ground, large enough to hold four of the inhabitants, with two or three ladders to mount it; from whence one of 20 them who seemed to be a person of quality, made me a long speech, of which I understood not one syllable.

I answered in a few words, but in a most humble manner, and being very weak from hunger, I could not help showing my impatience by putting my finger frequently to my mouth, to 5 show that I wanted food. The orator then got down from the stage, and commanded that several ladders should be set up against my sides. On these a hundred of the inhabitants mounted, and walked toward my mouth, carrying baskets 10 full of meat, which had been provided and sent thither by the king's orders.

I noticed there was the flesh of several animals, but could not distinguish them by the taste. There were shoulders, legs, and loins, shaped like 15 those of mutton, and very well dressed, but smaller than the wings of a lark. I ate them by two or three at a mouthful, and took three loaves of bread at a time, about the size of musket bullets. They supplied me as fast as they 20 could, showing a thousand marks of wonder at my appetite.

I then made another sign that I wanted drink. They found by my eating that a small quantity would not satisfy me, and slung up with great skill one of their largest hogsheads. They rolled it toward my hand, and beat out the top. I drank it off at a draught, which I might well do, for it did not hold half a pint. A second hogs-5 head I drank in the same manner, and made signs for more; but they had none to give me.

When I had performed these wonders, they shouted for joy and danced upon my breast. I confess I was often tempted, while they were pass-10 ing to and fro on my body, to seize forty or fifty of the first that came in my reach, and dash them against the ground. But I now considered my-self as bound by the laws of hospitality to a people who had treated me with so much kindness 15 and expense.

confused (kon fūzd'): not clear
creature (krē'chūr): a human being
draught (draft): the act of drinking
exhausted (egz ôst'ed): tired out
fastened (fas'nd): made firm
Gulliver (Gull'i ver)
hospitality (hŏs'pi tăl'i tў): kindness to a guest
jerkin (jer'kin): a short leather coat
Lilliput (Lill'i put)

mercy (mĕr'sў): kindness
quiver (kwĭv'er): a case for holding arrows
repeated (re pēt'ed)
succeeded (suk sēd'ed)
violent (vī'o lnt): fierce, severe
volley (vŏl'lў): a shower, as of arrows or stones
wrecked (rĕkt)
wrench (rench): to twist violently

II

After some time, when they observed that I made no more demands for food, there appeared before me a person of high rank from his imperial majesty. His excellency having mounted on 5 my ankle, came forward up to my face, with a dozen of his retinue, and spoke about ten minutes, pointing forward, which, as I afterward found, was toward the capital city, about half a mile distant. It was there that his majesty had ordered that I 10 must be conveyed. I made a sign with my hand that was loose, to show that I wanted my liberty. It appeared that he understood me, for he shook his head and held his hand in a position to show that I must be carried as a prisoner.

15 However, he made other signs to let me understand that I should have meat and drink enough, and very good treatment. Soon afterwards I heard a general shout, and I felt great numbers of people on my left side loosening the cords to 20 such a degree that I was able to turn upon my right side.

It seems that when I was found sleeping on
the ground, after my landing, the emperor had
news of it by a messenger, and he determined
that I should be tied while I slept, that plenty of
meat and drink should be sent me, and a machine 5
be prepared to carry me to the capital city.

This emperor has several machines fixed on
wheels for carrying trees and other great weights.
He often builds his largest men-of-war, some of
which are nine feet long, in the woods where 10
the timber grows, and has them carried on these
engines three or four hundred yards to the sea.
Five hundred carpenters and engineers were
immediately set at work to prepare the greatest
engine they had.   It was a frame of wood raised 15
three inches from the ground, about seven feet long
and four feet wide, moving on twenty-two wheels.

The shout I heard was upon the arrival of the
engine, which set out in four hours after my landing.   It was brought alongside me as I lay, but 20
the principal difficulty was to raise and place me
in this vehicle.   Eighty poles, each one foot high,
were set up for this purpose, and very strong

cords, of the bigness of coarse thread, were fastened
by hooks to many bandages, which the workmen
had tied round my neck, hands, body, and legs.
Nine hundred of the strongest men were em-
5 ployed to draw up these cords, by many pulleys
fastened on the poles, and thus, in less than three
hours, I was raised and slung into the engine,
and tied fast. All this I was told; for while
it was being done, I lay in a profound sleep.
10   Fifteen hundred of the emperor's largest horses,
each about four and a half inches high, were employed to draw me toward the metropolis, which
as I said was half a mile distant. We made a
long march during the remaining part of the day,
15 and rested at night with five hundred guards on
each side of me, half with torches and half with
bows and arrows, ready to shoot me if I moved.

The next morning at sunrise we continued our
march, and arrived within two hundred yards of
20 the city gate about noon. The emperor and all
his court came out to meet us; but his officers
would by no means allow his majesty to put himself in danger by mounting on my body.

GULLIVER IN LILLIPUT.

At the place where the carriage stopped, there stood an ancient temple, the largest in the whole kingdom, and in this building it was determined I should lodge. On each side of the gate was a small window, not more than six inches from the ground, and into the one on the left side, the king's smith conveyed four score and eleven chains (about as large as watch chains), which were locked to my left leg with six and thirty padlocks. When the workmen found it was impossible for me to break loose, they cut all the strings that bound me, whereupon I rose to my feet and looked about me.

I must confess that I never beheld a more entertaining view. The country around appeared like a garden, and the enclosed fields, which were generally forty feet square, looked like so many flower beds. Here and there between these fields were woods, the tallest trees of which appeared to be seven feet high. The town looked like the painted scene of a city in a theater.

The emperor now advanced on horseback and surveyed me with great wonder, but kept beyond the length of my chain. He ordered his cooks and butlers to give me food and drink, which they pushed forward in a sort of vehicle upon wheels. I took these vehicles and soon emptied them all. Twenty of them were filled with meat, 5 and ten with drink; each of the former afforded me two or three good mouthfuls, and I drank off the liquid at one draught. His imperial majesty spoke often to me, and I returned answers, but neither of us could understand a syllable. After 10 about two hours the court retired, and I was left with a strong guard.

ancient (ān′shnt) : very old

conveyed (kon vād′) : carried

enclosed (en klōzd) : surrounded by fences

engine (en′jĭn)

engineer (en gin ēr′) : one skilled in mechanics

entertaining (en ter tān′ing) : interesting and pleasing

excellency (ek′sel ln sy) : a title of honor

guard (gärd) : escort, protector

imperial (im pē′ri al) : royal

machine (ma shēn′)

men-of-war : ships for war

messenger (mes′sen jer)

metropolis (mē trop′ŏ lis) : the principal city

profound (pro found′) : deep

prospect (prŏs pect) : view

pulleys (pul′liz) : wheels over which ropes are run for lifting heavy weights

retinue (rĕt′i nū) : followers

score (skōr) : twenty

vehicle (vē′hĭ kl) : any sort of wagon or car for carrying things or people

III

Toward night I crept with some difficulty into
my house, where I lay on the ground. For
about a fortnight I slept there, while, by the
emperor's orders, a bed was being prepared for
5 me. Six hundred beds were brought in carriages,
and worked up in my house; a hundred and fifty
of the beds, sewn together, made up the breadth
and length, and these were of four thicknesses.
Even this, however, did not keep me from feeling
10 the hardness of the stone floor. In the same way,
they provided me with sheets, blankets, and coverlets, good enough for one who had been so long
used to hardships.

An establishment was also made of six hundred
15 persons to be my servants, and tents were built
for them very conveniently on each side of my
door. It was likewise ordered that three hundred
tailors should make me a suit of clothes, after the
fashion of the country; that six of his majesty's
20 greatest scholars should be employed to instruct
me in their language; and lastly, that the em-

peror's horses, and those of the nobility and troops of guards, should be frequently exercised in my sight, to accustom themselves to me.

All these orders were duly put in execution, and in about three weeks I made great progress in learning their language. During this time the emperor frequently honored me with his visits, and was pleased to assist my masters in teaching me. My gentleness and good behavior had gained so far on the emperor and his court, and indeed upon the army and people in general, that I began to conceive hopes of getting my liberty in a short time. I took all possible methods to win their confidence and good will. The natives came, by degrees, to be less fearful of any danger from me. I would sometimes lie down and let five or six of them dance over my head, and at last the boys and girls would venture to come and play hide-and-seek in my hair.

The horses of the army, having been daily led before me, were no longer shy, but would come up to my very feet without being startled. The riders would leap them over my hand, as I held it on the ground; and one of the emperor's huntsmen, upon a large courser, took my foot, shoe and all, which was indeed a wonderful leap.

I had sent so many petitions for my liberty, 5 that his majesty at length mentioned the matter, first in the cabinet, and then in full council, where it was opposed by none.

The first request I made after I had obtained my liberty was that I might have permission to 10 see Mildendo, the metropolis. This the emperor readily granted, but with a special charge to do no hurt either to the houses or inhabitants. The people were notified of my design to visit the town. The wall which encompasses it is two feet 15 and a half high, and at least eleven inches broad, so that a coach and horses may be driven very safely round it; and it is flanked with strong towers ten feet apart.

I stepped over the great western gate, and 20 passed very gently sideways through the two principal streets, wearing only my short waistcoat, for fear of damaging the roofs and eaves of the houses with the skirts of my coat. I walked with

the utmost care, to avoid treading on any strag-
glers who might remain in the streets, although
the orders were very strict that all people should
keep in their houses at their own peril.

The garret windows and tops of houses were so 5
crowded with spectators that I thought in all
my travels I had not seen a more populous place.
The city is an exact square, each side of the wall
being five hundred feet long. The two great
streets which run across and divide it into four 10
quarters are five feet wide. The lanes and alleys,
which I could not enter, but only viewed as I
passed, are from twelve to eighteen inches. The
town is capable of holding five hundred thousand
persons; the houses are from three to five stories 15
high, and the shops and markets are well provided.

The emperor had a great desire that I should
see his palace. By stepping over the buildings I
contrived to get into the inmost court; and then, 20
lying down upon my side, I looked in at the
windows of the middle stories. There I saw the
most splendid apartments that can be imagined.

The empress smiled at me from one of the windows and gave me her hand to kiss.

JONATHAN SWIFT: *Gulliver's Travels* (ADAPTED).

behavior (be hāv′yer) : conduct

cabinet (kăb′i net) : council

contrived (kon trīvd′) : managed

conveniently (kon vēn′yent lў)

council (koun′sil) : advisers

courser (kōrs′er) : a horse

coverlets (kuv′er lets) : light covers

difficulty (dif′fi kul tў)

encompass (en kum′p's) : to surround, to enclose

establishment (es tăb′lish mnt) : household, with servants

exercise (eks′er siz)

flanked (flankt) : protected at the side

Mildendo (Mil den′do)

nobility (nō bil′i tў) : men of rank

permission (per mish′un)

petition (pē tish′un) : request

sewn (sōn) : an old form for *sewed*

HELPS TO STUDY

I. 1. How did Gulliver come to Lilliput? 2. What did he first feel when he woke up? 3. What sort of creatures did he find around him? 4. What had they done to him? Why? 5. What did they do when he struggled?

II. 1. For what purpose were they building the platform? 2. How did they feed him? 3. Describe his interview with the king. 4. How did they get him to the city? 5. How big were their ships? 6. How many men and horses did it take to haul Gulliver to the city? 7. How did they bind him so he could not run away?

III. 1. How did they provide for the further care of him? 2. Tell how he came to win the confidence of the little people. 3. Tell about his visit to the principal city. 4. How did he get a view of the rooms of the emperor's palace? 5. Which of all the inventions of this story seem to you most amusing?

THE SEA

The sea, the sea, the open sea,
The blue, the fresh, the ever free!
Without a mark, without a bound,
It runneth the earth's wide regions round;
It plays with the clouds; it mocks the skies;   5
Or like a cradled creature lies.

I'm on the sea! I'm on the sea!
I am where I would ever be;
With the blue above, and the blue below,
And silence wheresoe'er I go;   10
If a storm should come and awake the deep,
What matter? I shall ride and sleep.

I love, oh, how I love, to ride
On the fierce, foaming, bursting tide,
When every mad wave drowns the moon,   15
Or whistles aloft his tempest tune,
And tells how goeth the world below,
And why the sou'west blasts do blow!

I never was on the dull, tame shore,
But I loved the great sea more and more,
And backward flew to her billowy breast,
Like a bird that seeketh its mother's nest;
5   And a mother she was and is to me;
For I was born on the open sea!

The waves were white, and red the morn,
In the noisy hour when I was born;
And the whale it whistled, the porpoise rolled,
10   And the dolphins bared their backs of gold;
And never was heard such an outcry wild
As welcomed to life the ocean-child!

I've lived since then, in calm and strife,
Full fifty summers a sailor's life,
15   With wealth to spend, and a power to range,
But never have sought, nor sighed for change;
And Death, whenever he comes to me,
Shall come on the wide, unbounded sea!

BARRY CORNWALL.

billowy (bil'lō y̆) : wavy
calm (käm) : quiet, peaceful
dolphin (dŏl'fin) : a sea animal
porpoise (por'pus) : a sea animal
range (rānj) : to wander or travel far

region (rē'jun) : realm, place
silence (sī'lns) : quiet
sou'west : southwest
wealth (wĕlth) : riches
whistles (hwis'lz)

HELPS TO STUDY

Since the beginning of English literature, more than a thousand years ago, there have been many poems about the joy of travel, and the fresh, free life of the sea. Remember that the English live on an island, and therefore must use the sea.

1. In the first stanza, what is meant by the third and fourth lines? 2. When does the sea play with the clouds? 3. When does it "lie like a cradled creature"? 4. In the second stanza, what is "the blue above, and the blue below"? 5. When is there silence on the sea? 6. In the third stanza, explain the third line. 7. What is the "tempest tune"? 8. In the fourth stanza, make the second line begin with "But that," and then tell what the first two lines mean. 9. Go to the dictionary and find out what porpoises and dolphins are. 10. Who is the "ocean-child"? Why? 11. Find lines that speak of the noise of the ocean. 12. Find lines that speak of its motion. 13. Where does the sailor show that he has no fear of the ocean? 14. Have you seen the ocean? Or a picture of it? If so, what do you remember about it?

c

SINDBAD'S SECOND VOYAGE

These stories of Sindbad are taken from *The Arabian Nights'*
Entertainment, a collection of strange stories brought into
Europe from the East. You may have read this or other won-
derful tales from this book.

I

I designed, after the first voyage, to spend the
rest of my days at Bagdad. But I soon grew
weary of an idle life, and put to sea a second
time, with merchants of known honesty.

5 We embarked on a good ship, and, after com-
mending ourselves to God, set sail. We traded
from island to island, and exchanged commodities
with great profit. One day we landed on an
island covered with several sorts of fruit trees,
10 but we could see neither man nor animal. We
walked in the meadows, along the streams that
watered them. While some of the company
amused themselves with gathering flowers and
others fruits, I took my wine and provisions,
15 and sat down near a stream between high trees
which formed a thick shade. I made a good

meal, and afterwards fell asleep. I cannot tell
how long I slept, but when I awoke the ship
was gone.

In this sad condition, I was ready to die with
grief. I cried out in agony, beat my head and[5]
breast, and threw myself upon the ground, where
I lay some time in despair.   I upbraided myself
a hundred times for not being content with the
profits of my first voyage, which might have
sufficed me all my life.   But all this was in vain,[10]
and my repentance came too late. At last I
resigned myself to the will of God.   Not knowing what to do, I climbed up to the top of a lofty
tree, from which I looked about on all sides to see
if I could discover anything that could give me[15]
hope.   When I gazed toward the sea I could
see nothing but sky and water; but looking over
the land I beheld something white; and coming
down, I took what provision I had left, and went
towards it, the distance being so great that I[20]
could not distinguish what it was.

As I approached, I thought it to be a white
dome of a prodigious height and extent; and

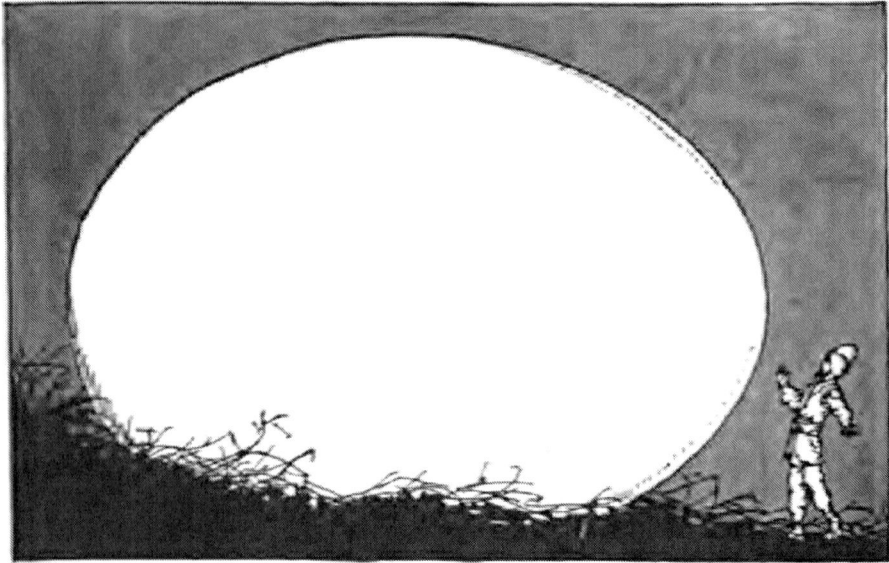

when I came up to it, I touched it and found it to be very smooth. I went round to see if it were open on any side, but saw it was not, and that there was no climbing up to the top, as it was so 5 smooth. It was at least fifty paces round.

By this time the sun was about to set, and all of a sudden the sky became as dark as if it had been covered with a thick cloud. I was much astonished at this sudden darkness, and still more 10 so when I found it caused by a bird of a monstrous size that came flying towards me. I remembered that I had often heard mariners speak

of a miraculous bird called the roc, and I was now
sure that the great dome which I so much ad-
mired must be its egg. And in fact, the bird
alighted and sat over the egg. As I perceived
her coming, I crept close to the egg so that I had 5
before me one of the legs of the bird, which was
as big as the trunk of a tree. I tied myself
strongly to it with my turban, in hopes that
the roc next morning would carry me with her
out of this desert island. After having passed the 10
night in this condition, the bird flew away as soon
as it was daylight, and carried me so high that I
could not discern the earth; she afterwards descended with so much rapidity that I lost my
senses. But when I found myself on the ground, 15
I speedily untied the knot, and had scarcely done
so when the roc, having taken up a serpent of a
monstrous length in her bill, flew away.

The spot where the bird left me was encom-
passed on all sides by mountains that seemed to 20
reach above the clouds, and so steep that there
was no possibility of getting out of the valley.
This was a new perplexity. When I compared

FIND SINDBAD.

this place with the desert island from which the roc had brought me, I found that I had gained nothing by the change.

As I walked through this valley, I perceived it was strewn with diamonds, some of which were of a surprising bigness. I took pleasure in looking upon them; but presently I saw at a distance what caused me extreme terror, — namely, a great number of serpents, so monstrous that the least of them was capable of swallowing an elephant. They retired in the daytime to their dens, where they hid themselves from the roc, their enemy, and came out only in the night.

agony (ag'o nўĭ) : great distress

approached (ap prōcht') : came up

commend (kŏm mĕnd') : to praise

commodities (kom mod'i tiz) : goods of various kinds

descend (de send') : to go or to come down

designed (de zīnd') : intended

discern (diz zĕrn') : to see

distinguish (dis tin̄'gwish) : to perceive

height (hīt) : altitude

mariners (măr'ĭ nerz) : sailors

miraculous (mi rak'ū lus) : wonderful and beyond belief

monstrous (mon'strus) : huge

perplexity (per pleks'i tўĭ) : doubt

provisions (pro vizh'uns) : food

prodigious (pro dij'us) : wonderful

rapidity (ra pid'i tўĭ) : speed

repentance (re pent'ns)

resigned (re zīnd') : submitted

sufficed (suf fīzd') : satisfied

turban (tûr'bn) : a head-gear worn in the East; a long piece of cloth wound round the head like a round cap

upbraided (up brăd'ed) : blamed, found fault with

voyage (voi'ăj) : a trip at sea

II

I spent the day in walking about the valley,
resting myself at times in such places as I
thought most convenient. When night came on
I went into a cave, where I thought I might re-
5 pose in safety. I secured the entrance, which
was low and narrow, with a great stone, to pre-
serve me from the serpents, but not so far as to
exclude the light. I supped on part of my provisions, but the serpents, which began hissing
10 round me, put me into such extreme fear that
I did not sleep. When day appeared the serpents left, and I came out of the cave trembling. I can justly say that I walked upon
diamonds without feeling any inclination to
15 touch them. At last I sat down, and, after
having eaten a little more of my provisions, fell
asleep in spite of my fears, for I had not closed
my eyes during the night. But I had scarcely
shut my eyes when something that fell by me
20 with a great noise, awaked me. This was a
large piece of raw meat; and at the same time

I saw several others fall down from the rocks in different places.

I had always regarded as fabulous what I had heard sailors and others relate of the valley of diamonds, and of the stratagems employed by [5] merchants to obtain jewels from thence; but now I found that they had stated nothing but the truth. For the fact is that the merchants come to the upper rim of this valley, when the eagles have young ones, and throw great joints of meat [10] into the valley; the diamonds, upon whose points they fall, stick to them; and the eagles, which are stronger in this country than anywhere else, pounce with great force upon those pieces of meat, and carry them to their nests on the [15] precipices of the rocks to feed their young. The merchants at this time run to their nests, disturb and drive off the eagles by their shouts, and take away the diamonds that stick to the meat.

I perceived in this device the means of my [20] deliverance.

Having collected together the largest diamonds I could find, and put them into the leather bag in which I used to carry my provisions, I took the largest of the pieces of meat, tied it close round me with the cloth of my turban, and then laid

myself upon the ground, with my face down-
5 wards, the bag of diamonds being made fast to my girdle.

I had scarcely placed myself in this posture when one of the eagles, having taken me up with the piece of meat to which I was fastened,
10 carried me to his nest on the top of the mountain.

The merchants immediately began their shouting to frighten the eagles; and when they had obliged them to quit their prey, one of them came to the nest where I was. He was much alarmed when he saw me, but he at once recovered himself, and [5] instead of inquiring how I came thither, began to quarrel with me and asked why I stole his goods. "You will treat me," replied I, "with more civility, when you know me better. Do not be uneasy. I have diamonds enough for you and [10] myself, more, indeed, than all the other merchants together. Whatever they have they owe to chance; but I selected for myself, in the bottom of the valley, those which you see in this bag."

I had scarcely done speaking, when the other [15] merchants came crowding about us, much astonished to see me; but they were much more amazed when I told them my story.

They conducted me to their encampment, and when they opened my bag, they were surprised at [20] the largeness of my diamonds, and confessed that they had never seen any of such size and perfection. I prayed the merchant who owned the

nest to which I had been carried (for every merchant had his own), to take as many for his share
as he pleased. He contented himself with one,
and that, too, the least of them; and when I
5 pressed him to take more, without fear of doing
me any injury, "No," said he, "I am very well
satisfied with this, which is valuable enough to
save me the trouble of making any more voyages,
and will bring me as great a fortune as I desire."

10   I spent the night with the merchants, to whom
I related my story a second time, for the satisfaction of those who had not heard it. I could not
moderate my joy when I found myself delivered
from the dangers I have narrated. I thought
15 myself in a dream, and could scarcely believe
myself out of danger.

From the *Arabian Nights*.

civility (sĭ vil′i tў̆) : politeness

deliverance (dē liv′er ans) : safety, rescue

device (dē vīs′) : design, plan

diamond (dī′a mund)

exclude (eks klūd′) : shut out

fabulous (fab′ū lus) : merely fanciful

frighten (frīt′′n)

inclination (in klĭ nā′shun) : wish

jewels (jū′els) : precious stones

moderate (mod′er ăt) : keep down

narrated (nar rāt′ed) : told

perfection (per fek′shun)

pounce (pouns) : to jump upon

precipices (pres′i pis es) : steep rocks

prey (prā) : food seized by animals

repose (re pōz') : rest

satisfaction (sat'is fak'shun)

secured (se kūrd') : fastened

stratagems (străt'a jems) : tricks

HELPS TO STUDY

I. 1. Where did Sindbad live? Tennyson has a fanciful poem about the splendors of Bagdad, called *Recollections of the Arabian Nights*. You might ask to have it read to you. 2. How did Sindbad get lost? 3. What does he tell about the roc's egg? 4. How did he get away from the island? 5. Where was he left? 6. What treasures and what danger did he find there?

II. 1. Describe Sindbad's adventure in the "valley of diamonds." 2. What preparation did he make for his escape? 3. How does the eagle aid in his escape? 4. Describe the meeting with the merchants. 5. With what good luck did he end this adventure?

The phrase "valley of diamonds" is often used to describe a fabulously rich place. Now you know what it means. In all your dreams of fortune, have you ever thought of any strange and marvelous ways of getting it?

Sindbad seems to have been a restless and busy fellow, as you may guess from what he said at the beginning of his story of his second voyage. In the original story he made seven voyages in all. In our next selection, his "Fifth Voyage," another strange thing happens to him in an uninhabited island, to which he has drifted, shipwrecked and alone.

SINDBAD'S FIFTH VOYAGE

I sat down upon the grass to recover myself from my fatigue, after which I went into the island to explore it. It seemed to be a delicious garden. I found trees everywhere, some of them
5 bearing green and others ripe fruits, and streams of fresh, pure water. I ate of the fruits, which I found excellent, and drank the water, which was very clear and good.

When I was a little advanced into the island,
10 I saw an old man who appeared very weak and infirm. He was sitting on the bank of a stream, and at first I took him to be one who had been shipwrecked like myself. I went towards him and saluted him, but he only slightly bowed his
15 head. I asked him why he sat so still, but instead of answering me, he made a sign for me to take him upon my back and carry him over the brook.

Believing him to be really in need of my assist-
20 ance, I took him upon my back. Having carried him over, I bade him get down, and stooped over

that he might get off with ease. But instead of
doing so (I laugh every time I think of it), the
old man, who to me appeared to be quite

decrepit, threw his legs nimbly about my neck.
He sat astride upon my shoulders, and held my 5
throat so tight that I thought he would have
strangled me, and I fainted away.

Notwithstanding my fainting, the ill-natured
old fellow still kept his seat upon my neck.
When I had recovered my breath, he thrust one 10

of his feet against my side, and struck me so
rudely with the other that he forced me to rise
against my will.   When I had arisen, he made me
carry him under the trees, and forced me now and
5 then to stop that he might gather and eat fruit.
He never left his seat all day; and when I lay
down to rest at night, he laid himself down with
me, still holding fast about my neck.   Every
morning he pinched me to make me awake, and
10 afterwards obliged me to get up and walk, and
spurred me with his feet.

One day I found several dry calabashes that
had fallen from a tree.   I took a large one, and,
after cleaning it, pressed into it some juice of
15 grapes, which abounded in the island; having
filled the calabash, I put it in a convenient place,
and going thither again some days after, I tasted
it and found the wine so good that it gave me
new vigor, and so exhilarated my spirits that I
20 began to sing and dance as I carried my burden.

The old man, perceiving the effect which this
had upon me, and that I carried him with more
ease than before, made me a sign to give him

some of it. I handed him a calabash, and as the liquor pleased his palate, he drank it off. There being a considerable quantity of it, he soon began to sing, and to move about from side to side in his seat upon my shoulders, and by 5 degrees to loosen his legs from about me.

Finding that he did not press me as before, I threw him upon the ground, where he lay without motion; I then took up a great stone and slew him.

From the *Arabian Nights.*

abounded (a bound'ed) : were plentiful

assistance (as sist'ns) : help

calabash (kăl'a bash) : a sort of gourd, hard and hollow

considerable (kon sĭd'er a bl)

decrepit (de krĕp'it) : feeble from old age

delicious (de lish'us) : pleasing to the taste

excellent (ex'sel nt) : very fine

exhilarate (egz ĭl'a rāt) : to cheer, to enliven

explore (eks plōr') : to look over a new or strange region

fatigue (fa tēg') : weariness

infirm (in fẽrm') : feeble

island (i'lnd)

obliged (ō blījd') : compelled

palate (păl'āt) : taste

quantity (kwŏn'ti tў) : amount

saluted (sa lūt'ed) : greeted, spoke to

HELPS TO STUDY

1. What did the old man at first seem to be ? 2. What did he get Sindbad to do ? 3. How did he keep him in real slavery ? 4. How did Sindbad get rid of him at last ?

You may have heard some burden or trouble that was hard to get rid of called " an old man of the sea." Now you know what the expression means and where it comes from.

D

ROBERT LOUIS STEVENSON

It was natural that Robert Louis Stevenson should write about travel, for he was a traveler nearly all his life. As a child he took imaginary journeys in his home at Edinburgh. He had all 5 sorts of adventures while he lay in bed or played about the garden. He was often ill, and not strong enough to play rough games. When he felt lonely he used to say to himself:

"The world is so great and I am so small,
10   I do not like it at all, at all."

But after a while he changed this saying into another, which you know:

"The world is so full of a number of things,
I'm sure we should all be as happy as kings."

15 Next to his father and mother Stevenson loved his nurse. She often danced and sang to amuse him, and she read poetry so wonderfully that he learned to care for beautiful words as if they were beautiful toys.

STEVENSON

From one place to another Stevenson was taken to improve his health. When he grew up he spent a great deal of time in France, which is a near neighbor of England and Scotland, as you know.
5 One of his most interesting journeys was in the south of France, in the company of a little donkey, which carried his food and his sleeping-bag. Some day you will read about his adventures in a book called *Travels with a Donkey*. He wrote another
10 travel-book about a journey in a canoe, partly in France and partly in Belgium. In two of his journeys he came to America, the first time to California and the second time to the Adirondacks, where he hoped to find good health.
15 Stevenson's longest journey was in the South Sea, where for more than three years he sailed about from one beautiful island to another. At last he built a house on a mountain side in Samoa, where the weather is always warm, and the birds
20 sing and the flowers blossom all the year round. He died there in 1894, only forty-six years old, and he was buried on the top of the mountain, by the dark-skinned natives who loved him. In one

of his poems, carved on his tombstone, he said, "glad did I live and gladly die."

Stevenson was tall and thin, his brown eyes were large and very bright, and all his movements were graceful. His hair was allowed to grow long 5 and he usually wore a velvet jacket. Although he was ill nearly all his life, no one was ever more cheerful and gay or enjoyed life more. He was kindly and sympathetic and could talk delightfully so that every one loved him. Once his wash- 10 woman's little son brought his pet canary "to amuse the sick gentleman." Stevenson is still loved and always will be, for he put himself into his books.

He liked to work. When he was so ill that he 15 could not read or even speak aloud, he wrote some of the poems in *A Child's Garden of Verses*. Besides poems and books of travel, he wrote many stories, long and short. One of the most interesting is *Treasure Island*, a pirate story full of ad- 20 venture written for boys. Girls enjoy it too.

TRAVEL

I should like to rise and go
Where the golden apples grow; —
Where below another sky
Parrot Islands anchored lie,
5   And, watched by cockatoos and goats,
Lonely Crusoes building boats; —
Where in sunshine reaching out
Eastern cities, miles about,
Are with mosque and minaret
10   Among sandy gardens set,
And the rich goods from near and far
Hang for sale in the bazaar; —
Where the Great Wall round China goes,
And on one side the desert blows,
15   And with bell and voice and drum,
Cities on the other hum; —
Where are forests, hot as fire,
Wide as England, tall as a spire,
Full of apes and cocoanuts
20   And the negro hunter's huts; —
Where the knotty crocodile

"AMONG THE DESERT SANDS
SOME DESERTED CITY STANDS."

Lies and blinks in the Nile,
And the red flamingo flies
Hunting fish before his eyes; —
Where in jungles, near and far,
5 Man-devouring tigers are,
Lying close and giving ear
Lest the hunt be drawing near,
Or a comer-by be seen
Swinging in a palanquin; —
10 Where among the desert sands
Some deserted city stands,
All its children, sweep and prince,
Grown to manhood ages since,
Not a foot in street or house,
15 Not a stir of child or mouse,
And when kindly falls the night,
In all the town no spark of light.
There I'll come when I'm a man
With a camel caravan;
20 Light a fire in the gloom
Of some dusty dining-room;
See the pictures on the walls,
Heroes, fights, and festivals;

And in a corner find the toys
Of the old Egyptian boys.

ROBERT LOUIS STEVENSON.

anchored (an'kerd): held securely

bazaar (ba zär') : an Eastern store

blinks : winks

caravan (kăr'a van): a company of people traveling on camels

cockatoo (kok'a tōō'): a kind of parrot

cocoanut (kō'kō nut'): a nut that grows on the palm tree

crocodile (krok'ō dīl): an animal with a horny skin

devour (dē vour'): to eat greedily

festival (fes'ti vl): celebration

flamingo (fla min'gō): a bird with long legs and bright red feathers

islands (i'lnds)

jungles (jun'glz): thick and tangled forests

minaret (mĭn'a ret): a slender pointed tower on a temple

mosque (mŏsk): a temple with a round dome for a roof

palanquin (pal'n kēn'): a litter in which a man is carried

HELPS TO STUDY

1. Which of the things mentioned in this poem would you most like to see? 2. In what countries would you expect to find them?   3. The Great Wall around China is a real wall, about 1500 miles in length, along the northern side of China. It was built more than 2000 years ago. 4. Why is the crocodile called "knotty"? 5. What is meant by the words, "the desert blows"? 6. Why are the cities said to "hum"? 7. What pictures does the boy expect to find in some deserted city? 8. What else does he think he may find there?

9. What things in your study of geography have made you want to travel? 10. As you read this poem through, see in your mind as many of the pictures as you can.

A MUNCHAUSEN ADVENTURE

I went on; night and darkness overtook me. No village was to be seen. The country was covered with snow, and I was unacquainted with the road.

5 Being tired, I alighted, and fastened my horse to something like a pointed stump of a tree, which appeared above the snow; for the sake of safety I placed my pistols under my arm, and lay down on the snow, where I slept so soundly that I did 10 not open my eyes till full daylight. Imagine my astonishment when I found myself in the midst of a village, lying in a churchyard. My horse was not to be seen; but presently I heard him neigh somewhere above. On looking upwards I 15 beheld him hanging by his bridle to the weathercock of the steeple. Matters were now very plain to me: the village had been covered with snow overnight; a sudden change of weather had taken place; I had sunk gently down to the churchyard 20 while asleep, as the snow had melted away; and

what, in the dark, I had taken to be a stump of a little tree appearing above the snow, to which I had tied my horse, proved to have been the cross or weather-cock of the steeple!

Without long consideration I took one of my 5 pistols, shot the bridle in two, brought down the horse, and proceeded on my journey.

RASPE : *Travels of Baron Munchausen.*

alighted (a lit'ed) : got down
neigh (nā)

proceeded (pro sēd'ed) : went on
unacquainted (un ak kwănt'ed)

HELPS TO STUDY

About a hundred and fifty years ago, Baron Raspe (pronounced Răs'pa), a German, wrote a book called *The Travels of Baron Munchausen.* In this book he made fun of the wild tales of travelers by telling a lot of lies even wilder and more ridiculous than any of them. This story is one of the best examples. You will notice the sober way in which he tells this thing, just as if it were an ordinary happening.

REVIEW QUESTIONS

1. Can you recall the title of the first selection? 2. Where was Lilliput? How large were the people there? How did they capture Gulliver? How did they feed him? 3. Where did you read about the Valley of Diamonds? What happened there? 4. Tell the story of Sindbad and the Old Man of the Sea. From what famous book is the story taken? 5. Who was Robert Louis Stevenson? Tell all you know about him. 6. What places and things does he say he wants to see in his poem, "Travel"? 7. What would the expression, "a Munchausen yarn" mean? 8. Which of the make-believe stories you have been reading is most interesting? 9. Which, if any, would you like to have happen to you? 10. What true tales of travel have you read?

JACK FROST

The Frost looked forth on a still, clear night,
And whispered, "Now, I shall be out of sight;.
So, through the valley, and over the height,
   In silence I'll take my way.
I will not go on like that blustering train,   5
The wind and the snow, the hail and the rain,
That make such a bustle and noise in vain;
   But I'll be as busy as they!"

So he flew to the mountain, and powdered its
   crest,
He lit on the trees, and their boughs he dressed
With diamonds and pearls; and over the breast
  Of the quivering lake he spread
A coat of mail, that it need not fear
The glittering point of many a spear
Which he hung on its margin, far and near,
  Where a rock could rear its head.

He went to the window of those who slept,
And over each pane like a fairy crept;
Wherever he breathed, wherever he stepped,
  By the morning light were seen
Most beautiful things! — there were flowers and
   trees,
There were bevies of birds and swarms of bees;
There were cities and temples and towers; and
   these
  All pictured in silvery sheen!

But he did one ring that was hardly fair, —
He peeped in the cupboard, and finding there

That all had forgotten for him to prepare.

"Now, just to set them a-thinking,

I'll bite this basket of fruit," said he,

"And this costly pitcher I'll burst in three!

And the glass of water they've left for me,   5

Shall 'tchick' to tell them I'm drinking."

HANNAH F. GOULD.

bevies (bĕv'iz) : flocks

bustle (bŭs'sl) : noisy motion

cupboard (kŭb'berd) : closet

margin (mär'jin) : edge, border

pearl (pĕrl) : precious stone

sheen (shēn) : gloss, glitter

whisper (hwis'per) : to speak softly

HELPS TO STUDY

A coat of mail was a suit of iron that soldiers wore in the days when they fought with swords and spears.

This old and familiar poem describes the frost in a playful manner. See if you can follow every trick and every wonder that the frost works.

1. How does the frost work; silently or noisily? 2. What is meant by the "blustering train"? 3. What did Jack Frost do to the mountain? To the trees? To the lake? 4. What did the frost do to the windowpanes? When you next see its work, see if you can find anything like these fanciful pictures. 5. What mischief was he guilty of in the kitchen?

THE FISH I DIDN'T CATCH

Yet, after all, I think the chief attraction of the brook to my brother and myself was the fine fishing it afforded us. Our bachelor uncle who lived with us was a quiet, genial man, much given to
5 hunting and fishing; and it was one of the great pleasures of our young life to accompany him to Great Hill, Brandy-brow Woods, the Pond, and,

best of all, to the Country Brook. We were quite willing to work hard in the cornfield or the hay-lot to finish the day's labor in season for an afternoon stroll through the woods and along the brookside.

I remember my first fishing excursion as if it were but yesterday. I have been happy many times in my life, but never more so than when I received that first fishing pole from my uncle's hand, and trudged off with him through the woods and meadows. It was a still sweet day of early summer; the long afternoon shadows of the trees lay cool across our path; the leaves seemed greener, the flowers brighter, the birds merrier than ever before. My uncle, who knew by long experience where were the best haunts of pickerel, considerately placed me at the most favorable point. I threw out my line as I had so often seen others do, and waited anxiously for a bite, moving the bait in rapid jerks on the surface of the water in imitation of the leap of a frog. Nothing came of it. "Try again," said my uncle. Suddenly the bait sank out of sight. "Now for it," thought I, "here is a

E

fish at last." I made a strong pull, and brought up a tangle of weeds. Again and again I cast out my line with aching arms, and drew it back empty. I looked to my uncle appealingly. "Try once more,"
5 he said. "We fishermen must have patience."

Suddenly something tugged at my line and swept off with it into deep water. Jerking it up, I saw a fine pickerel wriggling in the sun. "Uncle!" I cried, looking back in great excitement,
10 "I've got a fish!" "Not yet," said my uncle. As he spoke there was a plash in the water; I caught the arrowy gleam of a scared fish shooting into the middle of the stream; my hook hung empty from the line. I had lost my prize.

15 Overcome by my great and bitter disappointment, I sat down on the nearest hassock, and for a time refused to be comforted, even by my uncle's assurance that there were more fish in the brook. He refitted my bait, and, putting the pole again in
20 my hands, told me to try my luck once more.

"But remember, boy," he said, with his shrewd smile, "never brag of catching a fish until he is on dry ground. I've seen older folks doing that in

THE FISH I DIDN'T CATCH

more ways than one, and so making fools of themselves. It's no use to boast of anything until it's done, nor then either, for it speaks for itself."

How often since I have been reminded of the fish that I didn't catch! When I hear peoples boasting of a work as yet undone, I call to mind that scene by the brookside, and the wise caution of my uncle in that particular instance takes the form of a proverb: "Never brag of your fish before you catch him." 10

JOHN GREENLEAF WHITTIER.

accompany (ak kum′pa nĭ)

aching (āk′ing)

assurance (ă shur′ns) : confidence

genial (jēn′y al) : friendly

hassock (hăs′suk): a little raised place on the ground, covered with grass ; also called a hummock

instance (in′stns) : example

HELPS TO STUDY

Haunt of pickerel: a place where pickerel generally stay. The pickerel is a long, slender fish, much prized by fishermen in New England waters. This is the sort of story that makes every right-minded person want to go fishing.

1. What things show the beauty of the day, and of the landscape? 2. Explain "the arrowy gleam of a scared fish." 3. Whether the boy got any fish that day, he does not tell; ought he? 4. What advice did his uncle give? 5. What is the proverb about "counting chickens"?

A BOY'S SONG

Where the pools are bright and deep,
Where the gray trout lies asleep,
Up the river and o'er the lea,
That's the way for Billy and me.

5 Where the blackbird sings the latest,
Where the hawthorn blooms the sweetest,
Where the nestlings chirp and flee,
That's the way for Billy and me.

Where the mowers mow the cleanest,
Where the hay lies thick and greenest,
There to trace the homeward bee,
That's the way for Billy and me.

Where the hazel bank is steepest,   5
Where the shadow falls the deepest,
Where the clustering nuts fall free,
That's the way for Billy and me.

Why the boys should drive away
Little sweet maidens from the play,   10
Or love to banter and fight so well,
That's the thing I never could tell.

But this I know, I love to play,
Through the meadow, among the hay;
Up the water and o'er the lea,   15
That's the way for Billy and me.

JAMES HOGG.

---

banter (ban'ter) : to tease
hawthorn (hô'thôrn') : a rough,
  thorny bush, with a white flower
hazel (hā'zl) : the bush that bears
  the hazelnut

lea (lē) : an open field covered with
  grass
nestlings (nes'lings) : young birds
  in the nest

1. What things does this boy like? 2. Tell which
of them you have seen in your walks in the country.
3. What does " trace the homeward bee " mean? 4. What
things does this boy not like to do?

Notice that the last words in each pair of lines end in
the same sound; for example, " eep " in the first two,
" e " in the next two, and so on. These are called rhymes.
But there is one pair of lines in which the rhyme is not
perfect; find it.

THE WIND IN A FROLIC

The wind one morning sprang up from sleep,
Saying, "Now for a frolic! Now for a leap!
Now for a madcap, galloping chase!
I'll make a commotion in every place!"
5 So it swept with a bustle right through a great
town,
Creaking the signs, and scattering down
Shutters, and whisking, with merciless squalls,
Old women's bonnets and gingerbread stalls.
There never was heard a much lustier shout,
10 As the apples and oranges tumbled about;

And the urchins that stand with their thievish
    eyes
Forever on watch, ran off with each prize.

Then away to the field it went blustering and
    humming,
And the cattle all wondered whatever was coming;
It plucked by their tails the grave matronly cows, 5
And tossed the colts' manes all about their
    brows,
Till, offended at such a familiar salute,
They all turned their backs and stood silently
    mute.
So on it went capering and playing its pranks;
Whistling with reeds on the broad river-banks; 10
Puffing the birds as they sat on the spray,
Or the traveler grave on the king's highway.
It was not too nice to bustle the bags
Of the beggar and flutter his dirty rags.
'Twas so bold that it feared not to play its joke 15
With the doctor's wig and the gentleman's cloak.
Through the forest it roared, and cried gayly,
    " Now,

THE WIND IN A FROLIC.

72

You sturdy old oaks, I'll make you bow!"
And it made them bow without more ado,
Or it cracked their branches through and through.

Then it rushed like a monster o'er cottage and
    farm,
Striking their inmates with sudden alarm;   5
And they ran out like bees in a midsummer
    swarm.
There were dames with their kerchiefs tied over
    their caps,
To see if their poultry were free from mishaps;
The turkeys they gobbled, the geese screamed
    aloud,
And the hens crept to roost in a terrified crowd; 10
There was rearing of ladders, and logs laying
    on,
Where the thatch from the roof threatened soon
    to be gone.
But the wind had passed on, and had met in a
    lane
With a schoolboy, who panted and struggled in
    vain,

For it tossed him, and twirled him, then passed,
    and he stood
With his hat in a pool, and his shoe in the mud.

WILLIAM HOWITT.

commotion (kom mō'shun) : excitement

creaking (krēk'ing) : making a
squeaking noise

galloping (gal'lup ing)

gentleman (jen'tl mn)

kerchief (ker'chif) : a cloth tied
round the head

matronly (mā'trun lӯ) : motherly
and dignified

nice (nīs) : dainty, particular

offended (of fend'ed) : insulted

poultry (pōl'trӯ) : domestic fowls

terrified (ter'ri fīd) : frightened

thievish (thēv'ish) : sly, secret

threatened (thrĕt'nd) : warned

urchins (ur'chins) : small boys

HELPS TO STUDY

Rearing of ladders and logs laying on : putting up ladders
and laying logs on the thatched roof to keep the wind
from blowing it off

This poem is in the same spirit as "Jack Frost." The
wind is out for fun and mischief.

1. What does it do to the signs and the people in the
town? 2. What does it do to the animals on the farm?
3. What does it do to the trees in the forest? 4. Does
it do, or come near doing, any serious damage? 5. Tell
some of the pranks and some of the real harm that you
have known the wind to do. 6. Read the poem aloud
with life and spirit.

BROWNIE ON THE ICE

You would enjoy reading the whole book from which this story is taken. It begins this way: "There was once a little Brownie who lived — where do you think he lived? — in a coal-cellar." He was "only a little old man, about a foot high, all dressed in brown, with a brown face and hands, and a brown peaked cap, just the color of a brown mouse." He played all sorts of funny tricks, and was always the friend of the six children who lived in the house.

Devonshire is not very cold. Grass stays green and roses bloom there almost all year. So skating or sliding on ice is a great treat.

I

Winter was a grand time with the six little children, especially when they had frost and snow. This happened seldom enough for it to be the greatest possible treat when it did happen; and it never lasted very long, for the winters are warm 5 in Devonshire.

There was a little lake three fields off, which made the most splendid sliding place that ever was. No skaters went near it, it was not large enough; and besides, there was nobody to skate, the neigh- 10 borhood being lonely. The lake itself looked the

loneliest place imaginable.   It was not very deep, not deep enough to drown a man, but it had a gravelly bottom and was always very clear.   Also the trees round it grew so thick that they shel-
5 tered it completely from the wind; so when it did freeze, it generally froze as smooth as a sheet of glass.

One day the eldest boy ran in with a countenance of great delight.

10   "Mother, mother, the lake bears!"   (It was rather a compliment to call it a lake, it being only about twenty yards across and forty long.)   "The lake really bears!"

"Who says so?"

15   "Bill. Bill has been on it for an hour this morning, and has made us two such beautiful slides, he says — an up-slide and a down-slide. May we go to them directly?"

The mother hesitated.

20   "You promised, you know," pleaded the children.

"Very well, then; only be careful."

"And may we slide all day long, and never come home for dinner or anything?"

"Yes, if you like. Only Gardener must go with you, and stay all day."

This they did not like at all; nor, when Gardener was spoken to, did he.

"You bothering children! I wish you may all 5 get a good ducking in the lake! Serve you right for making me lose a day's work, just to look after you little monkeys. I've a great mind to tell your mother I won't do it."

But he did not, being fond of his mistress. He 10 was also fond of his work, but he had no notion of play. I think the saying of " All work and no play makes Jack a dull boy" must have been applied to him, for Gardener, whatever he had been as a boy, was certainly a dull and melancholy 15 man. The children used to say that if he and idle Bill could have been kneaded into one, and baked in the oven — a very warm oven —they would have come out rather a pleasant person.

As it was, Gardener was anything but a pleasant 20 person, above all to spend a long day with — and on the ice, where one needs all one's cheerfulness and good-humor to bear pinched fingers and numbed toes, and trips, and tumbles, and various uncomfortablenesses.

"He'll growl at us all day long — he'll be a regular spoil-sport!" lamented the children. "Oh! mother, mightn't we go alone?"

"No!" said the mother; and her "No" meant no, though she was always very kind. They argued the point no more, but started off, rather downhearted. But soon they regained their spirits, for it was a bright, clear, frosty day; the sun was shining, though not enough to melt the ice, and there was just sufficient frost to lie like a thin sprinkling over the grass, and turn the brown branches into white ones. The little people danced along to keep themselves warm, carrying between them a basket which held their lunch. A very harmless lunch it was, just a large brown loaf and a lump of cheese, and a knife to cut it with. Tossing the basket about in their fun, they managed to tumble the knife out and were having a search for it in the long grass when Gardener came up, grumpily enough. As they went they heard little steps pattering after them.

" Perhaps it is the Brownie coming to play with us — I wish he would," whispered the youngest girl to the eldest boy, whose hand she generally held; and then the little pattering steps sounded again, traveling through the snow, but they saw ₅ nobody—so they said nothing.

compliment (kom'pli ment)

countenance (koun'te nns): face, expression

Devonshire (Dev'n shēr): a county in the southern part of England

especially (es pesh'l lў)

gravelly (grăv'el lў): covered with pebbles or small stones

grumpily (grump'i lў): crossly

imaginable (im ăj'i na bl): that could be thought of

kneaded (nēd'ed): mixed together like dough

melancholy (mel'an kol ў): sober, sad

neighborhood (nā'ber hood)

no notion of play: no interest in play

sufficient (suf fish'nt): enough

II

The children would have liked to go straight to the ice; but Gardener insisted on taking them a mile round, to look at an extraordinary animal which a farmer there had just got — sent ·by his ₁₀ brother in Australia. The two old men stood gossiping so long that the children wearied extremely. Every minute seemed an hour till they got on the ice.

GARDENER CHASES THE KANGAROO.

By the time they reached the lake, Gardener was as cross as ever. He struck the ice with his stick, but made no attempt to see if it really did bear — though he would not allow the children to go one step upon it until he had tried. 5

Just then there was seen jumping across it a creature which certainly had never been seen on ice before. It made the most extraordinary bounds on its long hind legs, with its little fore-legs tucked up in front of it as if it wanted to 10 carry a muff, and its stiff tail sticking out straight behind to balance itself with, apparently. The children at first started with surprise, and then burst out laughing, for it was the funniest creature, and had the funniest way of getting along, that they 15 had ever seen in their lives.

" It's the kangaroo ! " cried Gardener in great excitement. " It has got loose — and it's sure to be lost — and what a way Mr. Giles will be in! I must go and tell him. Or stop, I'll try and 20 catch it."

But in vain — it darted once or twice across the ice, dodging him, as it were ; and once he came so

G

close that he nearly caught it by the tail — to the children's great delight — then it vanished.

"I must go and tell Mr. Giles directly," said Gardener, and then stopped. For he had promised not to leave the children — and it was such a wild-goose chase after an escaped kangaroo. But he might get half-a-crown as a reward, and he was sure of another glass of cider.

"You just stop quiet here, and I'll be back in five minutes," said he to the children. "You may go a little way on the ice — I think it's sound enough; only mind you don't tumble in, for there'll be nobody to pull you out."

"Oh, no," said the children, clapping their hands.

Off they darted, the three elder boys, with a good run; the biggest of the girls followed after them, and soon the whole four were skimming one after the other, as fast as a railway train, across the slippery ice. And like a railway train, they had a collision, and all came tumbling one over the other, with great screaming and laughter, to the high bank on the other side.

The two younger ones stood mournfully watching the others from the opposite bank — when there stood beside them a small brown man.

"Ho-ho! little people," said he, coming between them and taking hold of a hand of each. 5 His was so warm and theirs so cold, that it was

quite comfortable. And then somehow they found in their open mouths a nice lozenge — I think it was peppermint, but am not sure — which conforted them still more. 10

"Did you want me to play with you?" cried the Brownie. "Then here I am! What shall we do? Have a turn on the ice together?"

No sooner said than done. The two little children felt themselves floating along — it was more like floating than running — with Brownie between them, up the lake, and down the lake, and across the lake, not at all interfering with the sliders—indeed, 5 it was a great deal better than sliding. Rosy and breathless, their toes so nice and warm, and their hands feeling like mince pies just taken out of the oven — the little ones came to a standstill.

Australia (Aus trā'lya)

collision (col lĭzh'un) : bumping together

comfortable (kum'fert a ble)

dodging (dŏj'ing) : avoiding

extraordinary (eks trôr'di na rў̆) : strange, unusual

gossip (gŏs'sip) : idle conversation

half-a-crown : an English silver coin, worth about sixty cents

interfering (in'ter fēr'ing) : getting in the way of

kangaroo (kan'ga roo') : if you have never seen one, look in the dictionary for a picture of it.

lozenge (lŏz'enj)

mournfully (mōrn'ful lў̆) : sadly

reward (re wôrd') : pay, recompense

III

When all had had their fair turns, they began 10 to be frightfully hungry.

"Well," said Brownie, "what would you like to have? Let the little one choose."

She said, after thinking a minute, that she should like a currant cake.

"And I'd give you all a bit of it — a very large bit — I would indeed!" added she — almost with the tears in her eyes — she was so very hungry.

"Do it then!" said the Brownie in his little squeaking voice. Immediately the stone that the little girl was sitting on, a round hard stone and so cold! turned into a nice hot cake — so hot that she jumped up directly. As soon as she saw what it was, she clapped her hands for joy.

"Oh, what a beautiful, beautiful cake! only we haven't got a knife to cut it."

The boys felt in all their pockets, but somehow their knives never were there when they were wanted.

"Look! you've got one in your hand!" said Brownie to the little one; and that minute a bit of stick she held turned into a bread knife — silver, with an ivory handle — big enough, and sharp enough, without being too sharp. For the youngest girl was not allowed to use sharp knives, though she liked cutting things excessively, especially cakes.

"That will do. Sit you down and carve the

dinner. Fair shares, and don't let anybody eat too much. Now begin, ma'am," said the Brownie, quite politely, as if she had been ever so old.

Oh, how proud the little girl was! How 5 bravely she set to work! She cut five of the biggest slices you ever saw, and gave them to her brothers and sisters, and was just going to take the sixth slice for herself, when she remembered the Brownie.

10 "I beg your pardon," said she, as politely as he, though she was such a very little girl — and turned round to the wee brown man. But he was nowhere to be seen. The slices of cake in the children's hands remained cake, and uncom-15 monly good it was, and such substantial eating that it did nearly the same as dinner; but the cake itself turned suddenly to a stone again, and the knife into a bit of stick.

Just then they saw Gardener come clumping 20 along by the bank of the lake, and growling as he went.

"Have you got the kangaroo?" shouted the children, determined to be civil if possible.

"This place is bewitched, I think," said he. "The kangaroo was fast asleep in the cowshed. Now come away home."

It wasn't kind of Gardener, and I don't wonder the children felt it hard; indeed, the eldest resisted 5 stoutly.

"Mother said we might stop all day, and we will stop all day. You may go home if you like."

"I won't, and you shall!" said Gardener, smacking a whip that he carried in his hand. 10 "Stop till I catch you, and I'll give you this about your back, my fine gentleman."

And he tried to follow, but the little fellow darted across the ice — objecting to be either caught or whipped. It may have been rather 15 naughty, but I am afraid it was great fun, dodging Gardener up and down, he being too timid to go on the slippery ice, and sometimes getting so close that the whip nearly touched the lad. 20

"Bless us! there's the kangaroo again!" said he, starting. Just as he had caught the boy and lifted the whip, the creature was seen hop-hopping

from bank to bank. "I can't surely be mistaken
this time; I must catch it."

This seemed quite easy, for it limped as if it was
lame, or as if the frost had bitten its toes, poor
5 beast. Gardener went after it, walking cautiously
on the slippery, crackling ice, and never minding
whether or not he walked on the slides, though
they called out to him that his nailed boots would
spoil them.

10 But whether it was that ice which bears a boy
will not bear a man, or whether, at each lame step
of a kangaroo, there came a great crack, is more
than I can tell. However, just as Gardener reached
the middle of the lake, the ice suddenly broke and
15 in he popped — the kangaroo too, apparently, for
it was not seen afterwards.

What a hulla-balloo the poor man made! Not
that he was drowning — the lake was too shallow
to drown anybody; but he got terribly wet, and
20 the water was very cold. He soon scrambled out,
the boys helping him; and then he hobbled home
as fast as he could, not even saying thank you, or
taking the least notice of them.

Indeed, nobody took any notice of them — nobody came to fetch them, and they might have stayed sliding the whole afternoon. Only somehow they did not feel quite easy in their minds. And though the hole in the ice closed up imme-5 diately, and it seemed as firm as ever, still they did not like to slide upon it again.

"I think we had better go home and tell mother everything," said one of them. "Besides, we ought to see what has become of poor Gardener. 10 He was very wet."

"Yes; but oh, how funny he looked!" And they all burst out laughing at the recollection of the figure he cut, scrambling out through the ice with his trousers dripping up to the knees, and 15 the water running out of his boots, making a little pool wherever he stepped.

"Let's hope mother won't be vexed with us," said they, "but will let us come back again to-morrow. It wasn't our fault that Gardener tumbled in."   20

As somebody said this, they all heard quite distinctly, "Ha, ha, ha," and "Ho, ho, ho," and a sound of little steps pattering behind.

But whatever they thought, nobody ventured to say that it was the fault of the Brownie.

MULOCK: *Adventures of a Brownie* (ADAPTED).

clumping (klump'ing) : walking heavily

currant (kur'rnt) : a bush fruit

excessively (ek sĕs'iv lȳ) : very much indeed

frightfully (frīt'ful lȳ) : terribly

ivory (ī'vo rȳ)

recollection (rek ol lĕk'shun) : remembering .

resisted (re zist'ed) : held back, objected

stop (stŏp) : stay. (As used in England)

substantial (sub stăn'shl) : solid and satisfying

ventured (ven'tūrd) : dared

HELPS TO STUDY

I. 1. Why did Mother make Gardener go along? 2. How did he like it? 3. What is a "spoil-sport"?

II. 1. Where did they stop on the way? Why? 2. When do you first suspect that Brownie is going along? 3. What strange creature suddenly appeared on the ice? 4. What do you think it was really? 5. What did Gardener do?

III. 1. How did Brownie help the children enjoy themselves? 2. What happened when Gardener returned? 3. How did Brownie take a hand in the game again? 4. What finally happened to Gardener? 5. Were you sorry for him? 6. What is the last thing you hear of Brownie?

THE MOUNTAIN AND THE SQUIRREL

The mountain and the squirrel
Had a quarrel,
And the former called the latter "Little Prig."
Bunn replied:—
"You are doubtless very big,   5
But all sorts of things and weather
Must be taken in together
To make up a year
And a sphere.
And I think it no disgrace   10
To occupy my place.
If I'm not so large as you
You are not so small as I,
And not half so spry.
I'll not deny you make   15
A very pretty squirrel track.
Talents differ, all is well and wisely put.
If I cannot carry forests on my back,
Neither can you crack a nut."

RALPH WALDO EMERSON.

bunn or **bunny**: name given to a rabbit or a squirrel

disgrace (dis grās'): shame

doubtless (dout'less)

occupy (ok'kū pī): fill

prig: a person who thinks he is nicer than other people

quarrel (kwor'rel): dispute

sphere (sfēr): a ball, here meaning the earth

spry: active, quick

squirrel (skwer'rel)

talents (tăl'ntz): powers

HELPS TO STUDY

1. What name does the mountain call the squirrel? 2. When the squirrel "talks back," what does he say? 3. What is the last point he makes? 4. Which do you think gets the better of the argument? 5. Have you ever watched squirrels in the woods or in a city park? Did they seem dignified or frisky? 6. Why should the mountain call the squirrel a "prig"? 7. What things can a squirrel really do? 8. What things can the mountain do that are really useful? 9. The title that the author gave to this poem was "A Fable." Do you see why? 10. Three of the rhymes are not correct; find them.

REVIEW QUESTIONS

1. What tricks did Jack Frost play, and what beautiful things did he make?

2. What sort of creature was Brownie? How did he show himself friendly to the children?

3. What did the Mountain and the Squirrel talk about? What did they say?

TOM AND THE LOBSTER

This selection is from Kingsley's *Water-Babies*. Little Tom was a chimney-sweeper, overworked and cruelly treated. He was drowned in a river, changed into a "water-baby," and carried out to sea, where he saw and learned many strange things.

I

Tom was very happy in the water. He had been sadly overworked in the land-world; so now, to make up for that, he had nothing but holidays in the water-world for a long, long time to come. He had nothing to do now but enjoy himself, and 5 look at all the pretty things which are to be seen in the cool, clear water-world, where the sun is never too hot, and the frost is never too cold.

One day among the rocks he found a playfellow.

It was not a water-baby, alas! but it was a lob-10 ster, and a very distinguished lobster he was; for he had live barnacles on his claws, which is a great mark of distinction in lobsterdom, and no more to be bought for money than a good conscience or the Victoria Cross.   15

Tom had never seen a lobster before, and he was mightily taken with this one, for he thought him the most curious, odd, ridiculous creature he had ever seen; and there he was not far wrong, 5 for all the ingenious men, and all the scientific men, and all the fanciful men in the world, with all the old German bogy-painters into the bargain, could never invent, if all their wits were boiled into one, anything so curious, and so ridiculous, as 10 a lobster.

He had one claw knobbed and the other jagged; and Tom delighted in watching him hold on to the

seaweed with his knobbed claw, while he cut up
salads with his jagged one, and then put them into
his mouth, after smelling at them like a monkey.
And always the little barnacles threw out their
casting nets and swept the water, and came in for 5
their share of whatever there was for dinner.

But Tom was most astonished to see how
he fired himself off — snap! like the leap-frogs
which you make out of a goose's breastbone.
Certainly he took the most wonderful shots, and 10
backwards, too. For, if he wanted to go into a
narrow crack ten yards off, what do you think he
did? If he had gone in headforemost, of course
he could not have turned round. So he used to
turn his tail to it, and lay his long horns straight 15
down his back to guide him, and twist his eyes
back till they almost came out of their sockets, and
then made ready, present, fire, snap! — and away
he went, pop into the hole! and peeped out and
twiddled his whiskers, as much as to say, "You 20
couldn't do that."

Tom asked him about water-babies. "Yes,"
he said. "He had seen them often. But he did

not think much of them. They were meddlesome little creatures that went about helping fish and shells which got into scrapes. Well, for his part, he should be ashamed to be helped by little, soft 5 creatures that had not even a shell on their backs. He had lived quite long enough in the world to take care of himself."

He was a conceited fellow, the old lobster, and not very civil to Tom; and you will hear how he 10 had to alter his mind before he was done, as conceited people generally have. But he was so funny, and Tom so lonely, that he could not quarrel with him; and they used to sit in holes in the rocks and chat for hours.

alter (ạl'ter) : change

barnacles (bar'na klz) : tiny shellfish that fasten themselves to hard objects in the water

bogy-painters (bō'gy-pānt'erz): painters of dwarfs, elves, and so on

conceited (kon sēt'ed) : thinking too well of oneself

conscience (kon'shns) : sense of right or duty

distinguished (dis tin̰'gwisht) : famous

fanciful (fan'si ful) : imaginary

holidays (hol'i dāz)

ingenious (in jēn'yus) : clever, smart

knobbed (nŏbd) : rough

mightily (mĭt'i ly) : strongly

ridiculous (ri dik'ū lus) : absurd

scientific (sī en tif'ik) : agreeing with the rules of science

twiddled (twĭd'dld) : wiggled

Victoria Cross : an emblem or badge given in England for great bravery

II

One day Tom was going along the rocks in three-fathom water, when all of a sudden he saw a round cage of green withes, and inside it, looking very much ashamed of himself, sat his friend the lobster, twiddling his horns, instead of 5 thumbs.

"What! have you been naughty, and have they put you in the lockup?" asked Tom.

The lobster felt a little indignant at such a notion, but he was too much depressed in spirits 10 to argue; so he only said, "I can't get out."

"Why did you get in?"

"After that nasty piece of dead fish." He had thought it looked and smelt very nice when he was outside, and so it did, for a lobster; but now 15 he turned round and abused it because he was angry with himself.

"Where did you get in?"

"Through that round hole at the top."

"Then why don't you get out through it?" 20

"Because I can't;" and the lobster twiddled

his horns more fiercely than ever, but he was forced to confess.

"I have jumped upwards, downwards, backwards, and sideways, at least four thousand times, and I can't get out. I always get up underneath there, and can't find the hole."

Tom looked at the trap, and, having more wit than the lobster, he saw plainly enough what was the matter; as you may if you look at a lobsterpot.

"Stop a bit," said Tom. "Turn your tail up to me, and I'll pull you through hindforemost, and then you won't stick in the spikes."

But the lobster was so stupid and clumsy that he couldn't hit the hole. Like a great many fox-hunters, he was very sharp as long as he was in his own country; but as soon as they get out of it they lose their heads, and so the lobster, so to speak, lost his tail.

Tom reached and clawed down the hole after him till he caught hold of him; and then, as was to be expected, the clumsy lobster pulled him in headforemost.

"Hullo! here is a pretty business," said Tom.

"Now take your great claws and break the points
off those spikes, and then we shall both get out
easily."

"Dear me, I never thought of that!" said the
lobster; "and after all the experience of life that
I have had!"

You see experience is of very little good unless
a man, or a lobster, has wit enough to make use
of it.

But they had not got half the spikes away,
when they saw a great dark cloud over them;
and, lo and behold, it was the otter.

How she did grin and grin when she saw Tom.
"Yar!" said she, "you little, meddlesome wretch,
I have you now! I will serve you out for telling the salmon where I was!" And she crawled
all over the pot to get in.

Tom was horribly frightened, and still more
frightened when she found the hole in the top,
and squeezed herself right down through it, all
eyes and teeth. But no sooner was her head
inside than valiant Mr. Lobster caught her by
the nose and held on.

And there they were all three in the pot, roll-
ing over and over, and very tight packing it was.
And the lobster tore at the otter, and the otter
tore at the lobster, and both squeezed and
5 thumped poor Tom till he had no breath left in
his body; and I don't know what would have
happened to him if he had not at last got on
the otter's back, and safe out of the hole.

He was right glad when he got out, but he
10 would not desert his friend who had saved him;

and the first time he saw his tail uppermost he caught hold of it, and pulled with all his might.

But the lobster would not let go.

"Come along," said Tom, "don't you see she is dead?" And so she was, quite drowned and dead.

And that was the end of the wicked otter.

But the lobster would not let go.

"Come along, you stupid old stick-in-the-mud," cried Tom, "or the fisherman will catch you!" And that was true, for Tom felt some one above beginning to haul up the pot.

But the lobster would not let go.

Tom saw the fisherman haul him up to the boatside, and thought it was all up with him. But when Mr. Lobster saw the fisherman he gave such a furious and tremendous snap that he snapped out of his hand, and out of the pot, and safe into the sea. But he left his knobbed claw behind him, for it never came into his stupid head to let go after all; so he just shook his claw off as the easier method.

Tom asked the lobster why he never thought

of letting go. He said very determinedly that it was a point of honor among lobsters. And so it is.

KINGSLEY: *The Water-Babies.*

abused (a būzd′) : badly treated

clumsy (klum′zy) : awkward

depressed (de prest′) : downhearted, sad

desert (de zert′) : leave

experience (eks pē′ri ns)

fathom (făth′um) : six feet

indignant (in dĭg′nnt) : angry

lockup (lok′up) : jail

meddlesome (mĕd′d l sum)

naughty (nô′ty) : bad

otter (ŏt′ter) : a furred animal that lives in the sea

salmon (săm′un) : a kind of fish

tremendous (trē men′dus)

valiant (văl′yant): brave

withes (wĭths) : twigs, or sticks

HELPS TO STUDY

I. 1. Where did Tom live? 2. Describe his play-fellow. 3. What did the lobster think of Tom? 4. How did they pass the time? 5. Tell how the lobster went into the hole.

II. 1. What trouble did the lobster meet? 2. What danger was there before the fisherman came along? 3. How did Tom help the lobster? 4. How did the lobster get away before the fisherman got him? 5. Did you ever see a lobster with one or both claws gone? 6. What other animal can you name that hangs fast to things and won't let go? 7. What is it that the author says about the way to get good out of the experience that comes to us?

THE DAFFODILS

I wandered lonely as a cloud
  That floats on high o'er vales and hills,
When all at once I saw a crowd,
  A host, of golden daffodils,
Beside the lake, beneath the trees,   5
Fluttering and dancing in the breeze.

Continuous as the stars that shine
  And twinkle on the milky way,
They stretched in never-ending line
  Along the margin of the bay.   10
Ten thousand saw I at a glance,
Tossing their heads in sprightly dance.

The waves beside them danced, but they
  Outdid the sparkling waves in glee, —
A poet could not but be gay   15
  In such a jocund company.
I gazed, and gazed, but little thought
What wealth the show to me had brought.

For oft, when on my couch I lie,
  In vacant or in pensive mood,   20

They flash upon that inward eye
Which is the bliss of solitude;
And then my heart with pleasure fills,
And dances with the daffodils.

WILLIAM WORDSWORTH.

I wan - dered lone-ly as a cloud That floats on

high o'er vales and hills, . . When all at . once I saw a

crowd, A . host, of . gold-en daf - fo - dils, . .

Be - side the lake, be - neath the trees, .

Flut - tering and danc-ing in the breeze. Be - side the

lake, be-neath the trees, Flut-tering and danc-ing in the breeze.

continuous (kon tin'ū us) : going on and on

daffodils (dăf'fō dilz) : yellow, cup-shaped flowers

inward eye : the mind, the memory of things we have seen before

jocund (jŏk'und) : jolly

pensive (pen'siv): thoughtful and sad

solitude (sol'i tūd) : loneliness

sprightly (sprīt'lȳ) : lively

thousand (thou'znd)

vacant (vā'knt) : idle

HELPS TO STUDY

The poet has once seen these bright flowers by a lake. The sight gave him such joy that it was always a pleasure to remember the picture when it came to his mind.

1. In what way is a cloud "lonely"? 2. How did the poet feel before he saw the daffodils? 3. What words show their motion? 4. Read the lines, and see if they "dance." 5. Who is the poet that is meant in the third stanza? 6. Explain these expressions: "jocund company"; "vacant mood"; "pensive mood"; "bliss of solitude." 7. What "wealth" had the sight brought to the poet? Read the stanza that tells this.

THE SANDPIPER

Across the lonely beach we flit,
    One little sandpiper and I,
And fast I gather, bit by bit,
    The scattered driftwood, bleached and dry.
5 The wild waves reach their hands for it,
    The wild wind raves, the tide runs high,
As up and down the beach we flit,
    One little sandpiper and I.

Above our heads the sullen clouds
   Scud, black and swift, across the sky;
Like silent ghosts in misty shrouds
   Stand out the white lighthouses high.
Almost as far as eye can reach   5
   I see the close-reefed vessels fly,
As fast we flit along the beach,
   One little sandpiper and I.

I watch him as he skims along,
   Uttering his sweet and mournful cry;   10
He starts not at my fitful song,
   Nor flash of fluttering drapery.
He has no thought of any wrong,
   He scans me with a fearless eye;
Stanch friends are we, well tried and strong,   15
   The little sandpiper and I.

Comrade, where wilt thou be to-night,
   When the loosed storm breaks furiously?
My driftwood fire will burn so bright!
   To what warm shelter canst thou fly?   20
I do not fear for thee, though wroth

The tempest rushes through the sky;
For are we not God's children both,
Thou, little sandpiper, and I?

CELIA THAXTER.

A - cross the lone - ly beach we flit, One

lit - tle sand - pip - er and I, . . And fast I gath - er,

bit by bit, The scat - tered beach-wood, bleached and dry.

The wild waves reach their hands for it, The wild wind raves, the

tide runs high, As up and down the beach we flit, One

lit - tle sand - pip - er and I, . . As . . up and down the

beach we flit, One lit - tle sand - pip - er and I. . .

beach (bēch) : shore

bleached (blēcht) : made white

closereefed (klōs'rēft') : with sails drawn in

comrade (kom'rad) : companion

drapery (drā'per ў) : a fabric hung in loose folds and used for clothing or decoration

driftwood : wood that drifts up from the sea

fitful : coming now and then

furiously (fū'ri us lў) : madly

ghosts (gōsts) : spirits

loosed (loōst) : uncontrolled

scud (skŭd) : run swiftly

shroud : a wrapping for the dead

stanch (stȧnch) : firm

sullen (sŭl'ln) : cross, sulky

vessels (vĕs'selz) : ships

wroth (rôth) : angry, fierce

Helps to Study

1. If you did not know, how could you tell from the poem what the sandpiper is? 2. What picture does the first stanza give? The second? 3. Who are the only creatures on the lonely beach? 4. What things show that a storm is coming? 5. Where will the poet be to-night during the storm? 6. Where will the bird be? 7. Will it be safe and warm? 8. What does the last sentence in the poem mean? 9. How are the rhymes arranged in this poem? 10. Which lines sound best to you? Which do you like best?

THE FOUNTAIN

Into the sunshine,
  Full of the light,
Leaping and flashing,
  From morn till night;

5   Into the moonlight,
  Whiter than snow,
Waving so flower-like
  When the winds blow;

Into the starlight,
10   Rushing in spray,
Happy at midnight,
  Happy by day;

Ever in motion,
  Blithesome and cheery
15 Still climbing heavenward,
  Never aweary;

Glad of all weathers,
  Still seeming best,
Upward or downward,
20   Motion thy rest;

Full of a nature
    Nothing can tame,
Changed every moment,
    Ever the same;

Ceaseless aspiring,   5
    Ceaseless content,
Darkness or sunshine
    Thy element;

Glorious fountain,
    Let my heart be   10
Fresh, changeful, constant,
    Upward, like thee!

                        JAMES RUSSELL LOWELL.

aspiring (a spīr′ing): reaching up-   blithesome (blīth′sum): gay, happy
    ward

HELPS TO STUDY

Read this poem carefully to yourself; then read it aloud
in a lively way, that shows that you feel the rush and
dash of the water as it leaps and plays.

1. How does the fountain look in the sunlight?
2. In the moonlight? 3. In the fifth stanza, explain the
last line. 4. In the sixth stanza, what is said about the
nature of the fountain? 5. What lesson does the poet
wish to learn from the fountain?

In - to the sun - shine, Full of the light, . .

Leap - ing and flash - ing, From morn - ing till night;

In - to the moon - light, . Whit - er than snow, . .

Wav - ing so flow'r - like — When the winds blow.

THE NEW YEAR

Who comes dancing over the snow,
  His soft little feet all bare and rosy?
Open the door, though the wild winds blow,
  Take the child in and make him cosy.
  Take him in and hold him dear,
He is the wonderful glad New Year.

DINAH M. CRAIK.

THE BROWN THRUSH

"There's a merry brown thrush sitting up in a tree,
  He's singing to me! He's singing to me!"
And what does he say, little girl, little boy?
  "'Oh, the world's running over with joy!
    Don't you hear? Don't you see?   5
    Hush! Look! In my tree
  I'm as happy as happy can be!'"

And the brown thrush keeps singing: "A nest
    do you see,
  And five eggs, hid by me in the juniper-tree?
Don't meddle! don't touch! little girl, little boy, 10
  Or the world will lose some of its joy.

H

Now I'm glad! Now I'm free!
And I always shall be,
If you never bring sorrow to me."

So the merry brown thrush sings away in the
tree,
5 To you and to me, to you and to me;
And he sings all the day, little girl, little boy,
O, the world's running over with joy!
But long it won't be,
Don't you know? Don't you see?
⁾ Unless we are as good as can be!

LUCY LARCOM.

juniper (jū′ni per): an evergreen tree   lose (lōōz): to be deprived of

HELPS TO STUDY

1. The first stanza of the poem seems to be a conversation. Who are talking? 2. What is the spirit of the thrush's song, gay or sad? 3. Of what does he sing? 4. Read the poem freely and easily, and give the right feeling to it. Notice that if you read it quickly and freely, it is more like the song of the bird.

5. Stevenson has a poem called "Singing." Do you know it?

1. There's a mer - ry brown thrush sit - ting up . in a
And what does he say, lit - tle girl, lit - tle

tree, He's sing - ing to me, He's sing - ing to me."
boy? "O the world's . . run - ning o - ver with joy!

Don't you hear? Don't you see? Hush! Look! In my tree,
(2d verse) Now I'm glad! Now I'm free! And I al - ways shall be,
(3d verse) But . long it won't be, Don't you know? Don't you see?

In my tree, I'm as hap - py as hap - py can be!
If you nev - er bring sor - row, bring sor - row to me."
Un - less we're as good . as good as can be.

Review Questions

1. From what book is the story of "Tom and the Lobster" taken? Who wrote it? Who was Tom? What funny habits and ideas had he?

2. What lines can you recite from "The Sandpiper"? Describe the scene of the poem.

3. Of what things does the fountain make Lowell think? Find some lines in the poem that remind you of the motion of the fountain.

JOHN GREENLEAF WHITTIER

John Greenleaf Whittier was born on a farm in Haverhill (pronounced Hāv'er il), Massachusetts. The house was in a nest among the hills. The largest room was the kitchen, which was warmed 5 by a fireplace that took up nearly the whole of one side. When Whittier was small he went barefoot in summer time, fed the cows and the oxen, and did other work on the farm. He loved the beautiful hills. He knew all about the birds 10 and the wild-flowers, and the places where the nuts and the wild grapes ripened first. He knew where the muskrats lived and he hunted woodchuck holes.

In those days the country schools lasted for only 15 about three months every year, so that Whittier had little education in schools. But he read all the books he could get and read the Bible over and over. Always he kept reading good books, especially poetry, and soon he was writing both 20 prose and poetry himself. Whittier was a Quaker,

WHITTIER

117

and in his talk and letters used *thee* and *thy* instead of *you* and *your*.

When he was twenty-nine he left the old farm, and with his mother and sister Elizabeth settled ₅ down in the pleasant village of Amesbury, not far away. This was his home for the rest of his life. He was never strong. He lived an extremely quiet life. His best friend was his younger sister, Elizabeth, who resembled him in ₁₀ many ways.

We think of Whittier as the poet of the country life in New England. In " Snow Bound " he tells us how, when he was a boy, a great storm piled the drifts so high that he and his brother had to ₁₅ dig a tunnel to open the way to the barn. " The Barefoot Boy," on page 119, tells about Whittier's out-of-door pleasures when he was young, and a poem called " In School Days " is about a country school. In a beautiful poem named " Telling the ₂₀ Bees," he described the beehives on his father's farm, and in another, called " The River Path," he shows his love for the hills.

Whittier died in 1892, in his eighty-fifth year.

THE BAREFOOT BOY

Blessings on thee, little man,
Barefoot boy, with cheek of tan!
With thy turned-up pantaloons,
And thy merry whistled tunes;
With thy red lip, redder still   5
Kissed by strawberries on the hill;
With the sunshine on thy face,
Through thy torn brim's jaunty grace:
From my heart I give thee joy, —
I was once a barefoot boy!   10

O, for boyhood's painless play,
Sleep that wakes in laughing day,
Health that mocks the doctor's rules,
Knowledge never learned of schools,
Of the wild bee's morning chase,
Of the wild-flower's time and place,
How the tortoise bears his shell,
How the woodchuck digs his cell,
And the ground-mole sinks his well:
How the robin feeds her young,
How the oriole's nest is hung:
Where the whitest lilies blow,
Where the freshest berries grow.
For eschewing books and tasks,
Nature answers all he asks.
Hand in hand with her he walks,
Face to face with her he talks,
Part and parcel of her joy, —
Blessings on the barefoot boy!

O for boyhood's time of June,
Crowding years in one brief moon,
When all things I heard or saw,

Me, their master, waited for.
I was rich in flowers and trees,
Humming-birds and honey-bees;
For my sport the squirrel played,
Plied the snouted mole his spade;   5
For my taste the blackberry cone
Purpled over hedge and stone;
Laughed the brook for my delight
Through the day and through the night —
Whispering at the garden wall,   10
Talked with me from fall to fall;
Mine the sand-rimmed pickerel pond,
Mine the walnut slopes beyond,
Mine, on bending orchard trees,
Apples of Hesperides!   15
Still, as my horizon grew,
Larger grew my riches too;
All the world I saw or knew
Seemed a complex Chinese toy
Fashioned for a barefoot boy!   20

Oh for festal dainties spread,
Like my bowl of milk and bread —

Pewter spoon and bowl of wood.
On the doorsteps, gray and rude,
O'er me, like a regal tent,
Cloudy-ribbed the sunset bent.
5 Purple-curtained, fringed with gold,
Looped in many a wind-swung fold;
While, for music, came the play
Of the pied frogs' orchestra;
And, to light the noisy choir,
10 Lit the fly his lamp of fire.
I was monarch; pomp and joy
Waited on the barefoot boy!

Cheerily, then, my little man,
Live and laugh, as boyhood can!
15 Though the flinty slopes be hard,
Stubble-speared the new-mown sward,
Every moon shall lead thee through
Fresh baptisms of the dew;
Every evening from thy feet,
20 Shall the cool wind kiss the heat;
All too soon these feet must hide
In the prison cells of pride.

Lose the freedom of the sod,
Like a colt's, for work be shod,
Made to tread the mills of toil,
Up and down in ceaseless moil:
Happy if their track be found   5
Never on forbidden ground;
Happy if they sink not in
Quick and treacherous sands of sin;
Ah! that thou could'st know thy joy
Ere it passes, barefoot boy.   10

JOHN GREENLEAF WHITTIER:
The Barefoot Boy.

Bless-ings on thee, lit-tle man, Bare-foot boy with cheek of tan!
With thy turn'd up pant-a-loons, And thy mer-ry whis-tled tunes;

With thy red lip, red-der still, Kiss'd by straw-ber-ries on the hill;

With the sun-shine on thy face, Thro' thy torn brim's jaunty grace:
From my heart I give thee joy,—I was once a bare-foot boy.

dainties (dān'tiz) : good things

eschewing (es chū'ing) : throwing aside, rejecting

festal (fĕs'tal) : fit for a feast

Hesperides (Hes pĕr'ĭ dēz) : the fabled garden of the Gods ; a paradise

horizon (ho rī'zon) : where the earth and sky seem to meet

jaunty (jôn'tẙ) : gay, jolly

looped (loopt) : bent into loops

mocks : makes fun of

moil : hard work

monarch (mŏn'ark) : king

moon : month

orchestra (ôr'kes tra) : a band of musicians

oriole (ō'ri ōl) : a yellow and black bird, whose nest is like a pocket hanging on a branch of a tree

pied (pīd) : marked with two or more colors

pomp (pŏmp) : splendor

purpled : turned purple, ripened

regal (rē'gal) : kingly, royal

stubble-speared : full of sharp stalks of hay that has been cut

sward : meadow land

treacherous (trech'er us) : false, like a traitor

woodchuck : called groundhog in many places

Helps to Study

This is one of the best-known and best-loved poems in our language. Many a great man looks back, as Whittier did, to the time when he was a barefoot boy ; and many a boy, barefoot or shod, hopes to be a great man, as, perhaps, Whittier did. What ambition for the future have you ?

1. What pleasures has the boy ? 2. What things does he learn ? 3. Who is his teacher ? 4. Who is " part and parcel " of nature's joy ? 5. What is the meaning of " Apples of Hesperides ? " 6. Explain " prison cells of pride."

A HAPPY BOY

I

Bevis had wandered far into the woods, looking at this thing and talking to that, and utterly forgetful of time and distance. When, at length, he began to think of returning to the place where he had left his father loading hay, he found that 5 he did not know which way to go.

Just as he was thinking he would ask a bee to show him the way (for there was not a single bird in the woods), he came to a place where the oaks were thinner, and the space between them was 10 covered with bramble bushes. Here there were ripe blackberries, and soon his lips were stained with their juice. Passing on from bramble thicket to bramble thicket, by and by he shouted and danced and clapped his hands with joy, for there 15 were some nuts on a hazel bough, and they were ripe, he was sure, for the side toward the sun was rosy.

Out came his pocket knife, and with seven tremendous slashes, off came a branch with a crook. He crooked down a bough and gathered the nuts; there were eight on that bough, and on the next, four, and on the next, only two. But there was 5 another bough beyond, from which, in a minute, he had twenty more. He could not stay to crack them, but crammed them in his pocket and ceased to count.

"I will take fifty up to the squirrel," he said. 10 So he tugged at the boughs and dragged them down, and went on from tree to tree till he had gone very far into the nut-tree wood.

At last the thought came to him again that he would like to get out. So he stroked a knotted 15 oak with his hand, smoothing it down, and said, "Oak, oak, tell me which way to go."

The oak tried to speak; but there was no wind, and he could not. He dropped just one leaf on the right side, and Bevis picked it up, 20 and as he did so, a nut-tree bough brushed his cheek.

The bough could not speak, but it bent down towards a little brook. Bevis dropped on one knee and lifted up a little water in the hollow of his hand. He drank it, and asked which way to go.

The stream could not speak, because there was no stone to splash against; but it sparkled in the sunshine and looked so pleasant that Bevis followed it a little way. Soon he came to an open place with twisted old oaks, gnarled and knotted, where a blue butterfly was playing.

" Show me the way out, you beautiful creature," said Bevis.

" So I will, Bevis," said the butterfly. " I have just come from the field where your father is at work. He has been calling you, and I think he will soon be coming to look for you. Follow me, my darling."

So Bevis followed the little blue butterfly. Without pausing anywhere, but just zigzagging on, the butterfly floated before Bevis, and Bevis danced after him, the nuts falling from his crammed pockets. Presently he whistled to the butterfly to stop a moment while he picked a blackberry; the butterfly settled on a leaf.

Then away they went again together till they
left the wood behind and began to go up the hill.
There the butterfly grew restless, and Bevis could
scarcely keep with him. The child raced as fast
5 as he could go uphill, but at the top the butterfly
thought he saw a friend of his, and away he flew.

Bevis looked around. Everything was strange
and new to him. There were hills and fields
on every side, but not the field where he had
10 left his father. There was nothing but the
blue sky and the great sun, which did not seem
far off.

While he wondered which way to go, the wind
came along the ridge, and taking him softly by
15 the ear, said, "Bevis, my love, I have been waiting
for you ever so long. Why did you not come
before ? "

" Because you never asked me," said Bevis.

" Oh, yes, I did. I asked you twenty times in
20 the woods. I whispered to you from the nut
trees."

" Well, now I am come," said Bevis.   " But
where do you live ? "

"This is where I live, dear. I live upon the hill. Sometimes I go to the sea, and sometimes to the woods and sometimes I run through the valley; but I always come back here. And now I want you to romp with me." 5

"I will come," said Bevis. "I like a romp; but are you very rough?"

"Oh, no, dear; not with you."

"I am a great big boy," said Bevis. "I shall soon get too big to romp with you. How old 10 are you, you jolly wind?"

The wind laughed and said: "I am older than all the very old things. I am as old as the brook."

"The brook is very old," said Bevis. "He 15 told me he was older than the hills; so I do not think you are as old as he is."

"Yes, I am," said the wind. "He was always my playfellow. We were children together."

"If you are so very, very old," said the child, 20 "it is no use for you to romp with me, for I am strong. I can carry my papa's gun on my shoulder, and I can run very fast."

ɪ

BEVIS AND THE WIND.
130

"I can run quick," said the wind.

"But not so quick as I," said Bevis. "Now see if you can catch me."

am come: an expression formerly used for *have come*

Bevis (Bē'vis)

bramble (brăm'bl) : briers; a thorny vine or bush

forgetful (for get'ful)

gnarled (närld) : rough and twisted

juice (jūs)

knotted (nŏt'ed) : full of knots

valley (văl'lȳ)

zigzagging (zĭg'zăg'ging) : moving with sharp turns

II

Away he ran, and for a moment he left the wind behind. But the wind blew a little faster, and overtook him, and they raced along together like two wild things, till Bevis began to pant. Then down he sat on the turf and kicked up his heels and shouted, and the wind fanned his cheek and cooled him, and stroked his hair. Then Bevis jumped up again and danced along, and the wind helped him gently forward.

"You are a jolly old wind," said Bevis, "and I like you very much. But you must tell me a story, or we shall part. I'm sure we shall."

"I will try," said the wind, "but I have forgotten all my stories, because the people never come to listen to me now."

"Why don't they come?"

5 "They are too busy. They have so much to do that they have quite forsaken me."

"Well, I will come to you," said Bevis. "I will come and play with you."

"Yes, do," said the wind, "and drink me, 10 dear, as much as ever you can. I shall make you strong. Now drink me."

Bevis stood still and drew in a long, long breath. He drank the wind till his chest was full and his heart beat quicker. Then he jumped 15 and danced and shouted.

Then he lay down on the grass, and heard the wind whispering in the tufts and bunches; and the earth under him answered, and asked the wind to stay and talk.

20 But the wind said, "I have got Bevis to-day. Come on, Bevis"; and Bevis stood up and walked along.

"Now tell me, this instant," he said, "why the

sun is up there in the sky. Is he very hot if you touch him? Which way does he go when he sinks behind the wood? Who lives up there, and who painted the sky?"

The wind laughed aloud, and said: "Bevis, 5 my darling, you have not drunk half enough of me yet, else you would never ask such silly questions. Why, those are like the silly questions the people ask who live in the cities, and never feel me, or taste me, or speak to me. I have seen 10 them looking through long tubes —"

"I know," said Bevis, "they are telescopes. You look at the sun and the stars, and know all about them."

"Pooh!" said the wind. "Don't you believe 15 such stuff, my pet. How can they know anything about the sun, who never come up on the hills or go into the wood? How can they know anything about the stars, who never stopped on the hills all night? How can they who are 20 always shut up in houses know anything of such things?

"But Bevis, my love, if you want to know all

about the sun and the stars and everything, come to me and I will tell you.   In the morning, get up as quick as you can, and drink me as I come down the hill.   In the day go up on the hill, 5 and drink me again, and stay there, if you can, till the stars shine out.   And by and by you will understand all about the sun, and the moon, and the stars, and the earth, which is so beautiful. The more you drink of me the more you will 10 want, and the more I shall love you."

"Yes, I will drink you," said Bevis, "and I will shout.   Hello!"   And he ran up to the top of the little hill, and danced about on it, as wild as could be.

15 "Dance away, dear," said the wind, much delighted.   "Everybody dances who drinks me. Come, dear, let us race again."

So the two went on again and came to a hawthorn bush.   Then Bevis, full of mischief, tried 20 to slip away from the wind by running round the bush, but the wind laughed and caught him.

A little farther on, and they came to the old familiar field, and there Bevis saw his father busy

at work loading hay into the wagon. The field
was yellow with stubble, and the hills beyond
it and the blue valley were just the same as he
had left them.

Then the wind caressed him, and said: 5
"Good-by, darling. I am going yonder, straight
across to the blue valley and the blue sky, where
they meet. But I shall be back again when you
come next time. Now remember to drink me —
come up here and drink me." 10

"I will remember," said Bevis. "Good-by,
jolly old wind."

"Good-by, dearest," whispered the wind.

As Bevis went down the hill, a blue harebell,
that had been singing farewell to summer all 15
the morning, called to him and asked him to
gather her and carry her home, for she would
rather go with him than stay, now autumn was
so near.

Bevis gathered the harebell, and ran with the 20
flower in his hand down the hill; and as he ran,
the wild thyme kissed his feet and said, "Come
again, Bevis, come again."

At the bottom of the hill the wagon was standing, all loaded now. So his father lifted him up, and he rode home on the sweet, fragrant hay.

RICHARD JEFFRIES.

autumn (ô'tm): fall of the year

busy (biz'zȳ)

caressed (ka rest')

fragrant (frā'grnt)

harebell (hâr'bel'): a wild flower, whose blossom is shaped like a bell

listen (lĭs'n)

mischief (mĭs'chif)

telescope (tel'e skōp): an instrument through which one looks at far-away things to make them seem nearer and plainer

thyme (tīm): a sweet-smelling plant

HELPS TO STUDY

I. 1. What playmates had Bevis? 2. What question did he ask each? 3. How did the oak answer? The nut-tree? The brook? The butterfly? The wind? 4. With which ones did he talk?

II. 1. With which did Bevis spend the day? 2. What things did it tell him? 3. What does it mean to drink the wind and grow stronger? 4. What two poems have you read in this book that are like this lesson? 5. Tell about some experience of your own, when you have been off by yourself and enjoyed it. Was it in city or country? What did you do? Was it good to remember afterward? What good did you get out of it?

SEVEN TIMES ONE

There's no dew left on the daisies and clover,
  There's no rain left in heaven;
I've said my "seven times" over and over —
  Seven times one are seven.

I am old, so old I can write a letter;   5
  My birthday lessons are done;
The lambs play always; they know no better —
  They are only one times one.

O moon! in the night I have seen you sailing
  And shining so round and low;   10
You were bright, ah, bright! but your light is
    failing, —
  You are nothing now but a bow.

You, moon, have you done something wrong in
    heaven,
  That God has hidden your face?   15
I hope, if you have, you will soon be forgiven,
  And shine again in your place.

O velvet bee, you're a dusty fellow;
  You've powdered your legs with gold!   20

137

O brave marshmary buds, rich and yellow,
  Give me your money to hold!

And show me your nest with the young ones in it—
  I will not steal it away;
5 I am old! you may trust me, linnet, linnet,—
  I am seven times one to-day!

JEAN INGELOW.

clover (klō'vẽr)
daisies (dā'ziz)
forgiven (fŏr-gĭv'n) : pardoned
heaven (hĕv'n)
linnet (lĭn'nĕt) : a small green bird
  about the size of the English
  sparrow

marshmary (märsh'mãr'ȳ) : a yellow
  flower that grows in the fields
powdered (pow'dẽrd)
seven times : the table of sevens in
  multiplication
yellow (yĕl lõ)

HELPS TO STUDY

1. What time of day is it? Is it clear or cloudy?
2. What does the little girl mean by her "seven times"
that she has said? 3. What makes her think of the lambs
playing *always?* How do you read this line? 4. How
did the moon look? 5. Have you ever seen the moon by
day? 6. Why does the little girl think the moon hides
part of its face? 7. What does she call the bee? 8. Why
does she say the marshmary has money? Remember its
color. 9. And the linnet, what does she say to it? 10. Altogether, she is having an interesting birthday. What
happy holiday times can you remember and tell about?

THE BROOK

I come from haunts of coot and hern,
　　I make a sudden sally,
And sparkle out among the fern,
　　To bicker down a valley.

By thirty hills I hurry down　　　　　　　5
　　Or slip between the ridges,
By twenty thorpes, a little town,
　　And half a hundred bridges.

Till last by Philip's farm I flow
　　To join the brimming river;　　　　　10
For men may come, and men may go,
　　But I go on forever.

I chatter over stony ways,
　　In little sharps and trebles,
I bubble into eddying bays,　　　　　　15
　　I babble on the pebbles.

With many a curve my banks I fret
　　By many a field and fallow,

And many a fairy foreland set
  With willow-weed and mallow.

I chatter, chatter, as I flow
  To join the brimming river;
5 For men may come and men may go,
  But I go on forever.

I wind about, and in and out,
  With here a blossom sailing,
And here and there a lusty trout,
10   And here and there a grayling.

And here and there a foamy flake
  Upon me, as I travel
With many a silver waterbreak
  About the golden gravel.

15 And draw them all along, and flow
  To join the brimming river;
For men may come, and men may go,
  But I go on forever.

I steal by lawns and grassy plots,
20   I slide by hazel covers;

I move the sweet forget-me-nots
    That grow for happy lovers.

I slip, I slide, I gloom, I glance,
    Among my skimming swallows;
I make the netted sunbeams dance   5
    Against my sandy shallows.

I murmur under moon and stars
    In brambly wildernesses;
I linger by my shingly bars;
    I loiter round my cresses.   10

And out again I curve and flow
    To join the brimming river;
For men may come and men may go,
    But I go on forever.

ALFRED TENNYSON.

I come from haunts of coot and hern, I make a sud-den sal-ly, . . And spar-kle out a-mong the fern, To bick-er down the val-ley.

bicker (bĭk'er): to babble or quarrel

brimming (brĭm'mĭng): full

coot (kōōt): a water fowl; a marsh hen

cover (kŭv'er): clumps of bushes

eddying (ĕd'dȳ ing): making little waves

fallow (făl'lō): land not plowed

foreland (fōr'land): a cape or promontory

fret (frĕt): to carve out little curves and corners

grayling (grā'lĭng): a fish

haunts (hänts): places often visited

hern (hẽrn): a heron, a long-legged bird that lives near water

mallow (măl'lō): a wild flower

sharps and trebles: musical terms, meaning high or sharp sounds

shingly (shĭn'glȳ): gravelly

thorpe (thôrp): an old form for thorp, a village

waterbreak (wȯ'ter brăk)

HELPS TO STUDY

This song of the brook is very well known. 1. What beautiful pictures does it give? 2. What pleasant sounds? 3. Pick out some of the lines or stanzas that seem to run along just like the brook. 4. Certain lines are repeated over and over in a poem and are called a *refrain*. Find them here.

THE OWL

When cats run home and light is come,
　　And dew is cold upon the ground,
And the far-off stream is dumb,
　　And the whirring sail goes round,
　　And the whirring sail goes round;
　　　Alone and warming his five wits,
　　The white owl in the belfry sits.

ALFRED TENNYSON.

ROBERT OF LINCOLN

Robert of Lincoln is a grown-up sort of name given to the bobolink. The name bobolink is given to this bird because it sounds like his song.

Merrily swinging on brier and weed,
   Near to the nest of his little dame,
Over the mountain side or mead,
   Robert of Lincoln is telling his name:
      Bob-o'-link, bob-o'-link,
      Spink, spank, spink;   5
Snug and safe is this nest of ours,
Hidden among the summer flowers,
      Chee, chee, chee!

Robert of Lincoln is gayly dressed,
  Wearing a bright, black wedding coat;
White are his shoulders, and white his crest,
  Hear him call in his merry note:
5   Bob-o'-link, bob-o'-link,
      Spink, spank, spink;
Look what a nice new coat is mine;
Sure, there was never a bird so fine.
     Chee, chee, chee!

10 Robert of Lincoln's Quaker wife,
  Pretty and quiet, with plain brown wings,
Passing at home a patient life,
  Broods in the grass while her husband sings:
     Bob-o'-link, bob-o'-link,
15   Spink, spank, spink;
Brood, kind creature; you need not fear
Thieves and robbers while I am here.
     Chee, chee, chee!

Six white eggs on a bed of hay,
20 Flecked with purple, a pretty sight:
There as the mother sits all day,
  Robert is singing with all his might:

Bob-o'-link, bob-o'-link,
    Spink, spank, spink,
Nice good wife that never goes out,
Keeping house while I frolic about.
    Chee, chee, chee. 5

Soon as the little ones chip the shell,
    Six wide mouths are open for food;
Robert of Lincoln bestirs him well,
    Gathering seeds for the hungry brood:
    Bob-o'-link, bob-o'-link, 10
    Spink, spank, spink,
This new life is likely to be
Hard for a gay young fellow like me.
    Chee, chee, chee.

Robert of Lincoln at length is made 15
    Sober with work, and silent with care,
Off is his holiday garment laid,
    Half forgotten that merry air:
    Bob-o'-link, bob-o'-link,
    Spink, spank, spink, 20
Nobody knows but my mate and I,
Where our nest and our nestlings lie.
    Chee, chee, chee.

K

Summer wanes; the children are grown,
Fun and frolic no more he knows,
Robert of Lincoln's a hum-drum drone;
Off he flies, and we sing as he goes:
5   Bob-o'-link, bob-o'-link,
      Spink, spank, spink,
When you can pipe that merry old strain,
Robert of Lincoln, come back again.
      Chee, chee, chee.

WILLIAM CULLEN BRYANT.

Mer - ri - ly swing-ing on bri - er and weed, . .
O - ver the moun - tain side . or mead, . .

Near to the nest of his lit - tle dame,
Rob - ert of · Lin - coln is tell - ing his name:

"Bob - o' - link, bob - o' - link, Spink, spank, spink; . .

Snug and safe is this nest of ours, Hid-den a - mong the

sum - mer flow - ers, chee, ... chee, chee!"

bestir (be ster'): to be busy

broods (broōdz): sits on the eggs in the nest

crest: a bunch of feathers on the head

drone (drōn): a lazy fellow

frolic (frŏl'ik): to play

gayly (gā'lȳ): brightly

holiday garment: gay clothing

Lincoln (link'n)

mead (mēd): a meadow, grassland

patient (pā'shnt)

Quaker (kwāk'er): a member of the Society of Friends, who dress in sober colors

strain (strān): song, tune

thieves (thēvz)

wanes (wānz): passes by

Helps to Study

1. What other birds do you know that are named from their song? 2. What does Robert sing about? Compare "The Brown Thrush." 3. What is his color? 4. Why is his wife called a Quaker? 5. What are his duties soon to be? 6. Where will he go when summer is over? 7. It will interest you to find out who the reed-bird of North Carolina and the rice-bird of Louisiana are.

Review Questions

1. Tell something of the life of Whittier. What pleasures had his Barefoot Boy?

2. What things did you like best in the story of "A Happy Boy"?

3. Who is speaking in "Seven Times One"? What kind of day is it? What pictures did you get when you read it?

4. What lines in "The Brook" are often repeated? Find some lines that remind you of the motion of a brook. What pictures in the poem do you like best?

THE BLUE AND THE GRAY

By the flow of the inland river,
  Whence the fleets of iron have fled;
Where the blades of the grave-grass quiver,
  Asleep are the ranks of the dead.
5 Under the sod and the dew,
  Waiting the Judgment Day,
Under the one, the Blue,
  Under the other, the Gray.

These in the robings of glory,
10   Those in the gloom of defeat,

148

All of the battle blood gory,
   In the dusk of eternity meet:
Under the sod and the dew,
   Waiting the Judgment Day;
Under the laurel, the Blue,   5
   Under the willow, the Gray.

From the silence of sorrowful hours
   The desolate mourners go,
Lovingly laden with flowers,
   Alike for the friend and the foe: 10
Under the sod and the dew,
   Waiting the Judgment Day;
Under the roses, the Blue,
   Under the lilies, the Gray.

So with an equal splendor   15
   The morning sun rays fall,
With a touch impartially tender,
   On the blossoms blooming for all.
Under the sod and the dew,
   Waiting the Judgment Day;   20
Broidered with gold, the Blue,
   Mellowed with gold, the Gray.

So, when the summer calleth,
  On forest and field of grain,
With an equal murmur falleth
  The cooling drip of the rain:
5 Under the sod and the dew,
  Waiting the Judgment Day;
Wet with the rain, the Blue,
  Wet with the rain, the Gray.

Sadly, but not with upbraiding,
10   The generous deed was done.
In the storm of years that are fading
  No braver battle was won:
Under the sod and the dew,
  Waiting the Judgment Day;
15 Under the blossoms, the Blue,
  Under the garlands, the Gray.

No more shall the war cry sever,
  Or the winding rivers be red;
They banish our anger forever
20   When they laurel the graves of our dead:
Under the sod and the dew,
  Waiting the Judgment Day;

Love and tears for the Blue,
  Tears and love for the Gray.

FRANCIS MILES FINCH.

banish (băn'ish): drive away

broidered (broid'erd): adorned

defeat (de fēt')

desolate (des'o lāt): sad and lonesome

eternity (e ter'ni tẙ): the never-ending time after this life

generous (jĕn'er us): unselfish

impartially (im pär'shl lẙ): equally

inland (in'lnd)

judgment (jŭj'mnt): opinion, decision

laurel (lô'rel): an emblem of victory

sever (sĕv'er): separate

upbraiding (up brād'ing): faultfinding

willow (wĭl'lo): an emblem of grief

HELPS TO STUDY

Blue was the color of the uniforms of the Union soldiers; gray the color of the Confederates.

This poem puts tenderly and beautifully the hope that there will be no more bitter feeling between North and South. Both were brave, and both thought they were in the right.

At the fiftieth anniversary of the battle of Gettysburg the veterans of the North and the South, the Blue and the Gray, met and marched together on the battlefield; they ate together and talked of old times in perfect friendship and good humor. In this way they expressed the fine spirit of this poem.

THE SOLDIER'S REPRIEVE

"Dear Father:— When this reaches you I shall be in eternity. At first it seemed awful to me, but I have thought about it so much now that it has no terror. They say they will not
5 bind me, nor blind me, but that I may meet my death like a man. I thought, Father, it might have been on the field of battle for my country, and that, when I fell, it would be fighting gloriously; but to be shot down like a dog for
10 nearly betraying it — to die for neglect of duty! Oh, Father, I wonder the very thought does not kill me! But I shall not disgrace you. I am going to write you all about it, and when I am gone you may tell my comrades. I cannot now.
15 "You know I promised Jemmie Carr's mother I would look after her boy, and when he fell sick I did all I could for him. He was not strong when he was ordered back into the ranks, and the day before that night I carried all his
20 luggage, besides my own, on our march. Toward night we went on double-quick, and though the lug-

152

gage began to feel very heavy, everybody else was tired, too; and as for Jemmie, if I had not lent him an arm now and then, he would have dropped by the way.   I was all tired out when we came into camp, and then it was Jemmie's turn to be sentry, 5 and I would take his place; but I was tired too, Father.   I could not have kept awake if a gun had been pointed at my head, but I did not know it until — well, until it was too late.

"They tell me to-day that I have a short reprieve 10 — given to me by circumstances — 'time to write to you,' — our good Colonel says.   Forgive him, Father, he only does his duty; he would gladly save me if he could; and do not lay my death up against Jemmie.   The poor boy is broken-hearted, 15 and does nothing but beg and entreat them to let him die in my stead.

"I can't bear to think of Mother and Blossom. Comfort them, Father!   Tell them that I died as a brave boy should, and that, when the war is over, 20 they will not be ashamed of me, as they must be now.   God help me; it is very hard to bear! Good-by, Father!"

Late that night the door of the back stoop opened softly; a little figure glided out, and went down the footpath that led to the road by the mill. She seemed rather flying than walking, 5 turning her head neither to the right nor to the left, looking only now and then to Heaven, and folding her hands as if in prayer. Two hours later the same young girl stood at the Mill Depot watching the coming of the night train; and the 10 conductor, as he reached down to lift her into the car, wondered at the tear-stained face that was upturned toward the dim lantern he held in his hand. A few questions and ready answers told him all, and no father could have cared more 15 tenderly for his only child than he for our little Blossom. She was on her way to Washington to ask President Lincoln for her brother's life. She had stolen away, leaving only a note to tell her father where and why she had gone. She had 20 brought Bennie's letter with her; no good, kind heart like the President's could refuse to be melted by it. The next morning they reached New York, and the conductor hurried her on to Washington.

Every minute, now, might be the means of saving her brother's life. And so, in an incredibly short time, Blossom reached the capital, and hastened immediately to the White House.

The President had but just seated himself to his morning's task of looking over and signing important papers, when, without one word of announcement, the door softly opened, and Blossom, with downcast eyes and folded hands, stood before him. "Well, my child," he said, in his pleasant, cheerful tones, "what do you want so bright and early in the morning?" "Bennie's life, please, sir," faltered Blossom. "Bennie! Who is Bennie?" "My brother, sir. They are going to shoot him for sleeping at his post."

"Oh yes," and Mr. Lincoln ran his eye over the papers before him. "I remember. It was a fatal sleep. You see, child, it was at a time of special danger. Thousands of lives might have been lost for his culpable negligence."

"So my father said," replied Blossom gravely, "but poor Bennie was so tired, sir, and Jemmie so weak. He did the work of two, sir, and it was

"Bennie's Life, Please, Sir."

156

Jemmie's night, not his; but Jemmie was too tired, and Bennie never thought about himself, that he was tired too."

"What is this you say, child? Come here, I do not understand." And the kind man caught eagerly, as ever, at what seemed to be a justification of an offense.

Blossom went to him; he put his hand tenderly on her shoulder, and turned up the pale, anxious face toward his. How tall he seemed, and he was President of the United States, too! A dim thought of this kind passed through Blossom's mind, but she told her simple and straightforward story and handed Mr. Lincoln Bennie's letter to read. He read it carefully; then taking up his pen, wrote a few hasty lines, and rang his bell. Blossom heard this order given: " Send this dispatch at once."

The President then turned to the girl and said, " Go home, my child, and tell that father of yours, who could approve his country's sentence, even when it took the life of a child like that, that Abraham Lincoln thinks the life far too precious

to be lost.   Go back; or — wait until to-morrow.
Bennie will need a change after he has so bravely
faced death; he shall go with you."

"God bless you, sir," said Blossom.   And who
5 shall doubt that God heard and registered the
prayer?

Two days after this interview the young soldier
came to the White House with his sister.   He was
called into the President's private room, and a
10 strap was fastened upon the shoulder.   Mr. Lincoln
then said, "The soldier that could carry a sick
comrade's baggage, and die for the act so uncom-
plainingly, deserves well of his country."   Then
Bennie and Blossom took their way to their Green
15 Mountain home.   A crowd gathered at the Mill
Depot to welcome them back, and as Farmer
Owen's hand grasped that of his boy, tears flowed
down his cheeks, and he was heard to say fervently, "The Lord be praised!"

NEW YORK OBSERVER.

announcement (an nouns'mnt)

approve (ap prōōv') : agree with

awful (ô'ful) : terrible

circumstances (ser'kum stan sez)

comrades (kŏm'rads) : companions

culpable (kül'på bl) : wrong

disgrace (dis grās') : shame

entreat (en trēt) : beg

fervently (fer'vnt lȳ) : earnestly

incredibly (in krĕd'i blȳ) : unbelievable

justification (jus'ti fi kā'shun) : excuse

luggage (lug'găj) : baggage, pack

neglect (neg lekt') : negligence

negligence (neg'li jens) : carelessness

precious (presh'us) : dear

registered (rej'is terd) : noted

reprieve (re prēv') : a pardon or putting off of punishment

sentry (sen'trȳ) : the soldier who stands on guard while the others rest

straightforward (strāt'for'wrd) : honest

HELPS TO STUDY

This true story needs little explanation or comment. Only, it was this kind of thing in Lincoln that made one of our later Presidents, Theodore Roosevelt, say, in the hundredth year after Lincoln's birth, "no other good man was so great, and no other great man was so good."

1. Why is a sentry's duty so important? 2. Why had the boy failed in his duty? Was he to blame, do you think? 3. What would you have done in his place? 4. What would you have done if you had been in Lincoln's place? 5. What other generous action by some great man can you recall? 6. Which do you admire most in your favorite heroes: strength or kindness?

OLD IRONSIDES

Ay, tear her tattered ensign down!
  Long has it waved on high,
And many an eye has danced to see
  That banner in the sky;
5 Beneath it rung the battle shout,
   And burst the cannons' roar; —
The meteor of the ocean air
  Shall sweep the clouds no more.

Her deck — once red with heroes' blood,
10 Where knelt the vanquished foe,
When winds were hurrying o'er the flood
  And waves were white below —
No more shall feel the victor's tread,
  Or know the conquered knee; —
15 The harpies of the shore shall pluck
  The eagle of the sea!

O, better that her shattered hulk
  Should sink beneath the wave;
Her thunders shook the mighty deep,
20 And there should be her grave:

Nail to the mast her holy flag,
  Set every threadbare sail;
And give her to the god of storms,
  The lightning and the gale!

OLIVER WENDELL HOLMES.

conquered (kon′kerd) : vanquished
ensign (en′sīn) : flag
harpies (här′piz) : birds of prey
meteor (mē′te er) : shooting star

ocean (ō′shn)
threadbare (thred′bâr) : worn to the
  bare thread
vanquished (van′kwĭshd)

HELPS TO STUDY

The old gunboat *Constitution*, built in 1797, was nick-named "Old Ironsides." It was used in the naval battles with Great Britain in the War of 1812. In 1833 there was a plan to break up the old ship, because it had grown useless for war. Oliver Wendell Holmes, then only twenty-four years old, wrote this poem. It was printed in newspapers all over the country, and as a result the plan to destroy "Old Ironsides" was given up.

L

THE STORY OF GRACE DARLING

On the evening of Wednesday, the fifth of September, 1838, the steamship *Forfarshire* left Hull, with a cargo of iron for Dundee. The day had been quite fine, with a light breeze blowing from the
5 south; but on Thursday the weather changed altogether, and at midnight a fearful storm was raging around the whole north coast, the wind having shifted to the northwest.

On the morning of Friday, the 7th, a sloop from
10 Montrose, bound for South Shields, sighted a small boat struggling hard with the big waves, which every moment seemed about to swamp her. The sloop went to the rescue; and in spite of the heavy seas, the men in the little boat were
15 at last got on board.

They were seven in all; and they believed themselves to be all that were saved of the crew and passengers of the *Forfarshire*, which was then lying a total wreck on Longstone, one of the
20 Farne Islands.

While they were still in the Humber, and not

twenty miles from Hull, one of the *Forfarshire's* boilers was found to be leaking, but the captain would not turn back. He had it patched up as well as he could, and the vessel kept on her way, though very slowly, not passing between the 5 Farne Islands and the mainland till Thursday evening.

When the gale came on, the leak grew worse than ever, and very soon the other two boilers were found to have holes in them. Through 10 these the water rushed out almost as fast as it was pumped in, so filling the place with steam and hot water that the stokers could not get to the fires.

Still the steamer struggled on, though with great difficulty, for the sea was running very high 15 by this time. At midnight they were off St. Abb's Head, when the engineers reported that the engines had ceased to work. The ship rolled helplessly on the waves, and the rocky coast was not far off.

Sails were spread and the vessel was put round 20 so that she might run before the gale and keep off the rocks; and as the tide was flowing southward, she drifted fast with wind and tide. Torrents of rain were falling, and in spite of the wind there was a thick fog.

About three o'clock the noise of breakers was heard a little way ahead, and at the same time a ₅light was seen away to the left, shining faintly through the darkness. Then the crew knew that they were being driven on one of the Farne Islands.

Now these islands are a group of bare and lonely ₁₀rocks, off the coast of Northumberland. They are twenty in number, some only uncovered at low tide, and all standing like a rugged iron wall before any unlucky boat that may be driven on them. Even in calm weather and by daylight ₁₅seamen take care not to go near them.

The captain of the *Forfarshire* tried to head the ship for the channel which runs between the islands and the mainland. It would have been at best a poor chance; it was hopeless here, for the ₂₀vessel would not answer to her helm. On she drove in the darkness, nearer and nearer came the sound of the breakers, and those on board grew mad with fear and despair. Women wailed and shrieked; the captain's wife clung to him weeping; the crew lost all order and thought of nothing but their own safety.

Between half-past three and four with a grinding crash the ship was flung heavily against a 5 huge rock.

In the awful moments which followed, five of the crew managed to lower one of the boats and push off in her. The mate swung himself over the side, and reached her; and a passenger, rushing up 10 from the cabin, seeing the boat already three yards from the ship, cleared the space with a bound, and landed safely in her, though he nearly upset her with his weight. She righted however; and the seven men in her were, as already said, picked 15 up by a sloop from Montrose.

And the rest of the ship's company — what of them? Had they all gone down by that island crag, with never a hand stretched out to help them? 20

Hardly had the boat got away when the *Forfarshire* was struck by a huge wave which lifted her up bodily, and dashed her back right

upon the edge of the rock. She at once broke
in two pieces, the after part, with about twenty
passengers, the captain and his wife, being swept
right away into the black waters. The front
5 half was lifted up on the rock.

In the fore cabin was a poor woman with a
child in each arm. When the vessel struck, the
waves rushed into the cabin, but the mother,
crouched in a corner, kept her place. First one
10 and then the other child died from cold and fright,
and was swept out of sight by the cruel waves,
though the poor soul herself lived through all the
horrors of the night.

About a mile from Longstone, the island on
15 which the vessel struck, lies Brownsman. This is
the outermost of the Farne Islands, and the lighthouse stands on it. In 1838 the keeper of the
lighthouse was William Darling. He was an
elderly, almost an old, man; and the only other
20 people in the lighthouse were his wife and his
daughter Grace, a girl of twenty-two.

On the night of the wreck Grace was lying
awake, and heard the cries that came across the

wild waters.; but in the darkness they could do nothing.

At length the day broke, and in the gray morning light they could see, with the help of a glass, the wreck on Longstone Island, and could make 5 out figures moving on it.

Between the two islands a heavy sea was running, so that the passage would be very hard for even a good boat rowed by strong men. But the only boat on the lighthouse was a clumsy 10 jolly-boat, and the only crew an old man and a young girl to face an angry sea and a tide dead against them.

At first Darling would not undertake anything so dangerous, but Grace could not rest. There 15 were men in great peril on the other side of that rough mile of sea, and she could not stay where she was and see them die. So off they set, the old man taking one oar, the girl the other, and both rowing with all their strength through the waves, 20 which might at any minute swamp their boat or dash it on the rocks.

Even if they got the poor people off the wreck,

GRACE DARLING AND HER FATHER.

perhaps they could not get them back to the lighthouse. The tide was at the turn and would be against them on their homeward way; in fact, death seemed to face them on every side.

When they got near enough to Longstone, Darling jumped on the rock, and Grace quickly pulled away from it, and by rowing hard all the time managed to keep the boat from being stranded.

There were now only nine alive on the wreck, and it is hard to say how they were got safely into the boat, tired out and helpless as they were; but they were got into it at last, and two of the men saved helped to row the boat back to Brownsman, which was safely reached.

When, after several days, the storm abated, and an account of Grace's brave deed was printed, her praise was in all the newspapers and on all men's lips. Artists came from far to paint her portrait; poets wrote about her; she was offered twenty pounds a night to show herself in London. But she never could be got to see that she had done anything out of the ordinary; and she remained a simple, unspoiled girl to the end of her short life.

breakers (brăk'erz) : waves

cargo (kär'go) : a ship's freight

crag (krăg) : a steep rock

crouched (kroucht) : bent low

engineer (en'ji nēr')

helm (hĕlm) : steering-wheel

Hull (hŭl) : a seaport town on the eastern coast of England

Humber (hŭm'ber) : a river that empties into the sea at Hull

minute (min'it)

Northumberland (nôr thŭm'ber lnd) : a county in the north of England

passenger (pas'sen-jer)

portrait (por'trāt) : likeness

rescue (res'ku) : to save

rugged (rug'ged) : rough

sloop (slo͞op) : a small sailing-vessel

stokers (stōk'erz) : firemen

swamp (swŏmp) : to fill and sink

torrents (tor'rnts) : floods

HELPS TO STUDY

This is a true story.   And the name of Grace Darling has been ever since among the names of our real heroes.

1. Where did Grace Darling live?   2. What was her father's work?   3. What danger to the ship did she see? 4. What did she do to save the passengers?   5. How well did she succeed?   6. What reward had she?   7. What stories of bravery can you recall?   8. Imagine that you were on the *Forfarshire* and describe the rescue.

CAPTAIN SMITH AND POCAHONTAS

This is a story about a man whose life and adventures were as interesting as any story book. His name was Captain John Smith, and he was born in England over three hundred years ago. You will like to know something about him, [5] because he was one of the first Englishmen who came to live in this country.

After many adventures on sea and land, Captain John Smith set out with some men who were going to make their homes in Virginia. They [10] crossed the ocean and settled at a place which they called Jamestown, after the king of England.

At first these settlers had a hard time. They were not used to working in the fields; and Smith, who was one of their chief men, found it hard to [15] make them cut down trees and plant corn. They were often in need of food and always in danger of attacks from Indians.

One day Captain Smith started with an Indian guide to see the country and to look for food. He [20] was going along the forest path, when suddenly

an arrow whizzed through the air and the Indian
war-cry rang in his ears.

The woods seemed to be filled with savages.
Captain Smith saw that it would be useless to
5 resist them. So he let them drag him off to their
chief, the Powhatan.

Captain Smith was kept prisoner for some time.
Then it was decided that he should be killed.
The war clubs of the savages were already raised
10 over his head, when a little girl ran forward, threw
her arms about his neck, and begged them not to
kill him. This was Pocahontas, the daughter of
the Powhatan.

They tried to drag her away, but she begged
15 so hard for the white man's life that at last her
prayer was granted and Smith's life was spared.

The Powhatan became so fond of his white prisoner that he wished to adopt him as his son. Soon
the Indians allowed Captain Smith to go back to
20 his friends in Jamestown.

Once, when the Indians were again at war with
the settlers, Pocahontas came at night and warned
the white men that there was to be an attack.

When the savages came, they found the settlers ready to defend themselves.

Captain John Smith stayed in Virginia for a number of years, leading the settlers in the Indian fights and guiding them in their work. Then he 5 returned to England, and wrote books telling about his adventures.

Some years later he sailed again for America. This time he visited the northern coast, and gave the name of New England to that part of our coun- 10 try. He died in England at the age of fifty-two.

Pocahontas married John Rolfe, a young Englishman. With him she visited England, where she was treated as a young princess. And to-day there are boys and girls in Virginia who can 15 say that they are descended from Pocahontas, the Indian princess, who lived more than three hundred years ago.

Pocahontas (Pō'ka hon'tas)

Powhatan (pow'hă tan): an Indian word meaning great chief

prayer (prâr): petition, entreaty

savage (săv'ăj): an uncivilized man

settlers (set'lerz): colonists

Virginia (Ver jĭn'i a): named in honor of Elizabeth, the *virgin* queen

whizzed (whĭzd): flew swiftly

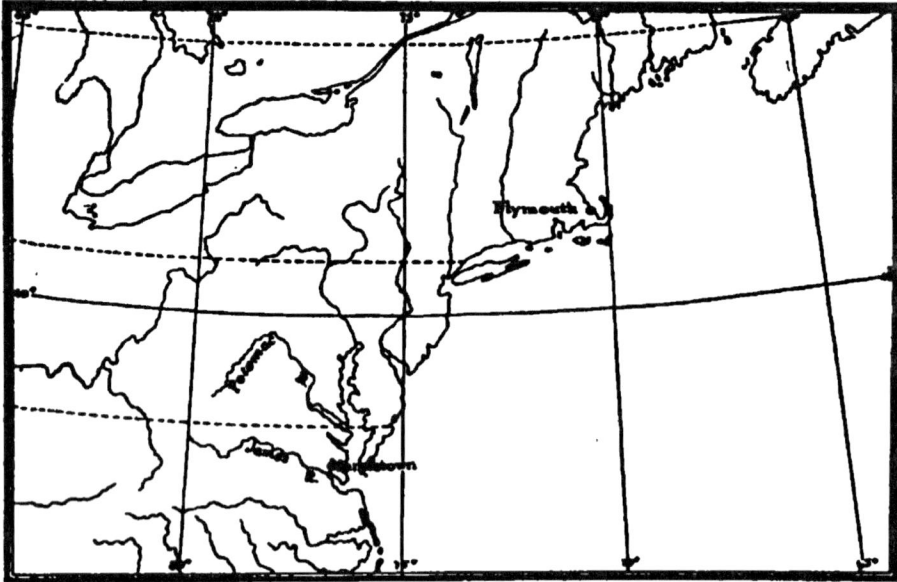

HELPS TO STUDY

This story is so famous that every boy and girl in the land is expected to know it. And yet, the students of history are not certain that it happened. Captain Smith was a brave and interesting man; but his accounts of his adventures do not always seem to be exact truth.

1. Does it tell about Jamestown and Captain John Smith in your history textbook? 2. What does it say? 3. Do you know what we mean by saying that Jamestown is the first permanent English settlement in America? 4. Did John Smith visit New England? 5. Where was the first permanent settlement made in New England? Who made it? 6. How does the story of Captain Smith differ from the stories of Imaginary Travels (pp. 11–61)?

THE JACK–O'–LANTERN

The children had been working busily all day helping their father and mother with the harvesting. It would soon be Thanksgiving Day, and the nuts had to be gathered and stored away, the pumpkins and corn put into the barn, and the apples cut, strung, and hung up to dry.

In the olden time, you see, the children had

to work during the spring planting and the fall harvesting, and they went to school a little in the winter and summer.

After supper the family gathered round the big ₅fireplace in the kitchen, — all but the father, who had gone to help a neighbor.

"Let us string a few more apples," said Endurance. "Father filled the baskets again this afternoon!"

₁₀ "Oh, no!" said Obed. "Let us make a jack-o'-lantern. I found a big yellow pumpkin and Father gave it to me."

"Yes, yes," cried all the children. "Let us make a jack-o'-lantern!" and they watched with ₁₅eager interest while Obed cut off the top of the pumpkin and scooped out the seeds.

"Now make two big eyes," said Endurance, and Obed cut two round holes in the rind. Then he cut a long narrow opening.

₂₀ "What a big mouth!" said Patience.

"The better to eat you with, my dear," said one of the boys, as Obed added a nose and two ears.

"Mother, Mother, may we have a candle? Our lantern is finished," cried the children at last.

Mrs. Moore found a bit of candle and lighted it. How the big eyes glared, and the mouth grinned! Truly, it was an ugly face. 5

Just then a man came riding by. "The Indians, the Indians!" he cried. "They are coming up from the swamp. There is not time for you to go to the blockhouse."

"Take the children, Mother," said Obed, "and 10 hide them in the loft. Amos and I will stay here and watch for the Indians, and perhaps Father will come soon to help us."

In a moment the children were hidden, the fire was covered, and the boys were peering out into 15 the darkness.

"Look, look!" whispered Amos, "there is a shadow behind that tree. I think it is an Indian." Then, as he saw the shadow move, he spoke again. "Let us try to scare him, Obed. The jack-o'-lan- 20 tern, quick!"

The jack-o'-lantern was lighted and set in the window. It moved its head from side to side. It

M

glared and stared into the night. It disappeared and appeared again.

The Indian saw its shining eyes, its grinning mouth, and he fled through the woods in terror.

5 "The fire spirit! The fire spirit!" he called to his comrades, and they hurried with him back to the swamp.

All night long Obed kept the jack-o'-lantern in the window, but the Indians never dared to return 10 to the abode of the great fire spirit.

blockhouse (blok'hous): a strong house, built of logs, for defense

eager (ē'ger): earnest

fireplace: a part of the chimney so constructed that a fire can be built in it

neighbor (nā'ber)

Obed (Ō'bed): a Bible name taken from the Hebrew language. It means *worshiper.*

pumpkin (pump'kin)

terror (ter'rer): fright

HELPS TO STUDY

Endurance: the Puritans often named their children after some good quality. Patience, Virtue, and Faith are names often used. Names from the Bible were also often used.

This story takes us back to the old colony days in New England where the Puritans were making a settlement.

1. What have you read in your history about the Puritans? About the Indians? 2. What is the fire spirit?

BENJAMIN FRANKLIN

Benjamin Franklin, the youngest in a family of seventeen children, was born in Boston in 1706. His father was a poor candle-maker, so the boy was put to work at the age of ten years. He learned the printer's trade, working for one of his elder brothers. At seventeen he decided to strike out for himself, going to Philadelphia, where he soon became a successful printer. When he was forty years old, he gave up his business in order to gain time for study and for service to his country.

After Franklin left school he continued to study, mastering Latin and French, and learning much about mathematics and science.

At the time the Colonies were struggling with Great Britain for their independence, Franklin was one of the first citizens of this country. He helped to draw up the Declaration of Independence and was one of the signers. He was sent to Europe, where he won friends for the American cause. Upon his return to this country, he was highly honored and served the government in many capacities.

FRANKLIN

FRANKLIN'S FIRST DAY IN PHILA-DELPHIA

I have been the more particular in this descrip
tion of my journey, and shall be so of my first
entry into that city, that you may in your mind
compare such unlikely beginnings with the figure
I have since made there. I was in my working 5
dress, my best clothes being to come round by

sea. I was dirty from my journey, my pockets were stuffed out with shirts and stockings, and I knew no soul nor where to look for lodgings. I was fatigued with traveling, rowing, and want of rest. I was very hungry, and my whole stock of cash consisted of a Dutch dollar, and about a shilling in copper. The latter I gave the people of the boat for my passage, who at first refused it on account of my rowing; but I insisted on their taking it. A man is sometimes more generous when he has but a little money than when he has plenty, perhaps through fear of being thought to have but little.

Then I walked up the street, gazing about till near the market-house I met a boy with bread. I had made many a meal on bread, and, inquiring where he got it, I went immediately to the baker's he directed me to, in Second Street, and asked for biscuit, meaning such as we had in Boston; but they, it seems, were not made in Philadelphia. Then I asked for a three-penny loaf, and was told they had none such. So not considering or knowing the difference of money, and the greater cheapness nor the names of his bread, I bade him give me three-penny worth of any sort. He gave me, accordingly, three great puffy rolls. I was surprised at the quantity, but took it, and, having no room in my pockets, walked off with a roll under each arm, and eating the other. Thus I went up Market Street as far as Fourth Street, passing by the door of Mr. Read, my future wife's father; when she, standing at the door, saw me, and thought I made, as I certainly did, a most 10 awkward, ridiculous appearance. Then I turned and went down Chestnut Street and part of Walnut Street, eating my roll all the way and, coming round, found myself again at Market Street wharf, near the boat I came in, to which I went 15 for a draught of the river water; and, being filled with one of my rolls, gave the other two to a woman and her child that came down the river in a boat with us, and were waiting to go farther.

Thus refreshed, I walked again up the street, 20 which by this time had many clean-dressed people in it, who were all walking the same way. I joined them, and thereby was led into the great meeting-

house of the Quakers near the market. I sat down among them, and, after looking round awhile and hearing nothing said, being very drowsy through labor and want of rest the preced-
5 ing night, I fell fast asleep, and continued so till the meeting broke up, when one was kind enough to rouse me. This was, therefore, the first house I was in, or slept in, in Philadelphia.

FRANKLIN: *Autobiography.*

Dutch dollar: a Dutch coin called Daalder (dah′ler), worth about thirty cents

entry (en′try) : going into

fatigued (fa tēgd′) : tired

particular (par tik′u ler) : careful of the little things

Quaker: one who belongs to the Society of Friends, a religious denomination

refreshed (re fresht′): made stronger

ridiculous (rĭ dik′u lus) : laughable

shilling (shil′ling): an English coin worth nearly twenty-five cents

HELPS TO STUDY

1. What things show that Franklin was poor? 2. What shows that he was successful later on? 3. Describe his appearance. Who noticed him as he walked up the street? 4. Where did he first sleep in Philadelphia, and how did he come to be there? 5. Of what other self-made men have you heard?

TURNING THE GRINDSTONE

When I was a little boy, I remember, one cold winter's morning, I was accosted by a smiling man with an ax on his shoulder. "My pretty boy," said he, "has your father a grindstone?" "Yes, sir," said I. "You are a fine little fellow,"5 said he, "will you let me grind my ax on it?" Pleased with the compliment of "fine little fellow," "O yes, sir," I answered. "It is down in the shop." "And will you, my man," said he, patting me on the head, "get me a little hot10 water?" How could I refuse? I ran, and soon

brought a kettle full. "How old are you? and
what's your name?" continued he, without waiting for a reply. "I am sure you are one of the
finest lads that ever I have seen; will you just
5 turn a few minutes for me?"

Tickled with the flattery, like a little fool, I
went to work, and bitterly did I rue the day. It
was a new ax, and I toiled and tugged till I was
almost tired to death. The school-bell rang, and
10 I could not get away; my hands were blistered,
and the ax was not half ground. At length,
however, it was sharpened; and the man turned
to me with, "Now, you little rascal, you've played
truant; scud to the school, or you'll rue it!"

15 "Alas!" thought I, "it was hard enough to turn
the grindstone, this cold day; but now to be called
a little rascal, is too much."

FRANKLIN : *Autobiography*.

HELPS TO STUDY

1. How was Franklin fooled into doing the man's work
for him? 2. What lesson did he learn from this experience? 3. What does the common saying, "a man with
an ax to grind" mean?

TOO DEAR FOR THE WHISTLE

When I was a child of seven years old, my friends, on a holiday, filled my pocket with coppers. I went directly to a shop where they sold toys for children; and being charmed with the sound of a whistle, that I met by the way, in the hands of another boy, I voluntarily gave all my money for one. I then came home, and went whistling all over the house, much pleased with my whistle, but disturbing all the family. My brothers, and sisters, and cousins, understanding the bargain I had made, told me I had given four times as much for it as it was worth; put me in mind of what good things I might have bought with the rest of the money, and laughed at me so much for my folly that I cried with vexation; and the reflection gave me more chagrin than the whistle gave me pleasure.

This, however, was afterwards of use to me, for the impression continued on my mind, so that often, when I was tempted to buy some unnecessary thing, I said to myself, " Don't give too

much for the whistle," and I saved my money.
As I grew up, came into the world, and observed
the actions of men, I thought I met with many,
very many, "who gave too much for the whistle."
5 When I saw one too ambitious of court favor,
sacrificing his time in attendance on levees, his
repose, his liberty, his virtue, and perhaps his
friends, to attain it, I have said to myself — "This
man gives too much for his whistle." When
10 I saw another fond of popularity, constantly
employing himself in political bustles, neglecting
his own affairs, and ruining them by neglect, "He
pays, indeed," said I, "too dear for his whistle."

If I knew a miser who gave up every kind of
15 comfortable living, all the pleasure of doing good
to others, all the esteem of his fellow-citizens,
and the joys of benevolent friendship, for the sake
of accumulating wealth — "Poor man," said I,
"you pay too dear for your whistle." When I
20 met a man of pleasure, sacrificing every laudable
improvement of the mind, or of his fortune, to
mere corporeal sensation, and ruining his health
in its pursuit, "Mistaken man," said I, "you are

providing pain for yourself, instead of pleasure; you are paying too dear for your whistle." If I see one fond of appearance or fine clothes, fine houses, fine furniture, fine equipages, all above his fortune, for which he contracts debts, "Alas," says I, "he has paid dear, very dear, for his whistle." In short, the miseries of mankind are largely due to their false estimate of things, — to giving "too much for their whistles."

FRANKLIN : *Autobiography.*

accumulating (ak kū'mu lăt ing): piling up

ambitious (am bish'us): wanting more honor

attendance on (at ten'dans): presence at

benevolent (be nev'o lent): kindly

contract debts (kon trakt' děts): to run into debt

coppers: the large copper pennies that were once used in this country, and still are in England

corporeal sensation (kor pō're al sen-sā'shun): pleasures of the body, like eating and drinking

court levees (kōrt lev'ēz): social gatherings at the court of a king

equipage (ek'wi pāj): carriage and horses

false estimates (fals es'ti māts): bad judgments, wrong ideas of what a thing is worth

laudable (laud'a bl): right, worthy of praise

sacrificing (sac'ri fīz ing): giving away, wasting

vexation and chagrin (veks ā'shŭn sha grin'): He was sorry and cross with himself for being so foolish.

voluntarily (vol'un ta'rily): of one's own free will

HELPS TO STUDY

This story explains itself: what does it mean?

THE MILLER OF THE DEE

There dwelt a miller, hale and bold,
 Beside the river Dee;
He worked and sang from morn till night—
 No lark more blithe than he;
5 And this the burden of his song
 Forever used to be:
"I envy nobody—no, not I—
 And nobody envies me!"

"Thou'rt wrong, my friend," said good King Hal,
10 "As wrong as wrong can be;
For could my heart be light as thine,
 I'd gladly change with thee.
And tell me now, what makes thee sing,
 With voice so loud and free,
15 While I am sad, though I'm a king,
 Beside the river Dee?"

The miller smiled and doffed his cap,
 "I earn my bread," quoth he;
"I love my wife, I love my friend,
20 I love my children three;

I owe no penny I cannot pay,
 I thank the river Dee
That turns the mill that grinds the corn
 That feeds my babes and me."

"Good friend," said Hal, and sighed the while, 5
 " Farewell, and happy be;
But say no more, if thou'dst be true,
 That no one envies thee;
Thy mealy cap is worth my crown;
 Thy mill my kingdom's fee;   10
Such men as thou are England's boast
 O miller of the Dee!"

CHARLES MACKAY.

Theredwelt a mil - ler, hale and bold, Be - side the riv - er Dee;

He worked and sang from morn till night, No lark more blithe than he; . And

this the bur - den of his song For ev - er used to be: . I

en - vy no - bod-y—no, not I—And no - bod-y en - vies me.

blithe (blith): gay, happy

burden (bur'dn): the part of a song
  that comes in again and again

doffed (doft): took off

hale (hāl): strong and well

the Dee: a river in the western part
  of England

Helps to Study

1. What was the "burden" of the miller's song?
2. Why was he so happy? 3. Why did the king envy
him? 4. Why does he call the miller's cap "mealy"?
5. What does he mean by saying that such men are
"England's boast"?

Review Questions

1. Who was Grace Darling? Where did she live?
What brave thing did she do? 2. Who was Captain
John Smith? Tell the story of Pocahontas. 3. What is
a jack-o'-lantern? Tell how some children once saved
their lives with one. 4. Tell all you can about Franklin's
useful life. Tell about his first day in Philadelphia. Explain the saying, "to pay too dear for the whistle." Tell
the story of "the man with an ax to grind." 5. What
made the Miller of the Dee such a happy man?

THE FAIRIES OF THE CALDON-LOW

There are many old stories in England and Ireland of the good deeds and the naughty pranks of the fairies. This poem tells of their kindness to people who needed help. The Caldon-Low was one of the places where the fairies used to gather for their dances by night.

"And where have you been, my Mary,
    And where have you been from me?"
"I've been to the top of the Caldon-Low,
    The midsummer night to see!"

"And what did you see, my Mary,   5
    All up on the Caldon-Low?"
"I saw the blithe sunshine come down,
    And I saw the merry winds blow."

"And what did you hear, my Mary,
    All up on the Caldon Hill?"   10
"I heard the drops of water made,
    And I heard the corn-ears fill."

"Oh, tell me all, my Mary —
    All, all that ever you know;
For you must have seen the fairies   15
    Last night on the Caldon-Low."

"Then take me on your knee, mother,
   And listen, mother of mine:
A hundred fairies danced last night,
   And the harpers they were nine.

5 "And their harp-strings sung so merrily,
   And their dancing feet so small;
But oh! the sound of their talking
   Was merrier far than all."

"And what were the words, my Mary,
10   That you did hear them say?"
"I'll tell you all, my mother,
   But let me have my way.

"And some they played with the water,
   And rolled it down the hill;
15 'And this,' they said, 'shall speedily turn
   The poor old miller's mill;

"'For there has been no water
   Ever since the first of May;
And a busy man shall the miller be
20   By the dawning of the day!

"'Oh, the miller, how he will laugh,
    When he sees the mill-dam rise!
The jolly old miller, how he will laugh,
    Till the tears fill both his eyes!'

"And some they seized the little winds,   5
    That sounded over the hill,
And each put a horn into his mouth,
    And blew so sharp and shrill!

"'And there,' said they, 'the merry winds go,
    Away from every horn;   10
And those shall clear the mildew dank
    From the blind old widow's corn:

"'Oh, the poor blind widow —
    Though she has been blind so long,
She'll be merry enough when the mildew's gone, 15
    And the corn stands stiff and strong!'

"And some they brought the brown linseed,
    And flung it from the Low:
'And this,' said they, 'by the sunrise,
    In the weaver's croft shall grow!   20

"'Oh, the poor lame weaver!
  How he will laugh outright
When he sees his dwindling flax-field
  All full of flowers by night!'

5 "And then upspoke a brownie,
  With a long beard on his chin:
'I have spun up all the tow,' said he,
  'And I want some more to spin.

"'I've spun a piece of hempen cloth,
10 And I want to spin another;
A little sheet for Mary's bed
  And an apron for her mother.'

"And with that I could not help but laugh,
  And I laughed out loud and free;
15 And then on the top of the Caldon-Low,
  There was no one left but me.

"And all on the top of the Caldon-Low
  The mists were cold and gray,
And nothing I saw but the mossy stones
20 That round about me lay.

"But, as I came down from the hill-top,
   I heard, afar below,
How busy the jolly old miller was,
   And how merry the wheel did go!

"And I peeped into the widow's field,
　And, sure enough, was seen
The yellow ears of the mildewed corn
　All standing stiff and green!

5 "And down by the weaver's croft I stole,
　To see if the flax were high;
But I saw the weaver at his gate
　With the good news in his eye!

"Now, this is all that I heard, mother,
10　And all that I did see;
So, prithee, make my bed, mother,
　For I'm tired as I can be!"

MARY HOWITT.

brownie: a kind of fairy that was supposed to do work in the night for the people he liked

Caldon-Low: a hill in central England

corn-ears: in England, corn means wheat or rye, not maize as in this country

croft (krôft): a very small farm

dank: damp

dwindling (dwin'dling): dying

low (lō): a small hill

linseed: the seed of the flax

midsummer night: on the night of June twenty-first the fairies were all supposed to be out

mildew (mil'dū): a growth found on decaying plants

mill-dam rise: water rising in the dam

prithee (prith'e): old form for *I pray thee*

tow (tō): flax not yet spun

"And where have you been, my   Ma - ry,   And
"I've been to the top   of the Cal - don - Low, The

where have you been from me?   And where have you been from me?"
mid - summer's night to see,   The mid-sum-mer's night to see!"

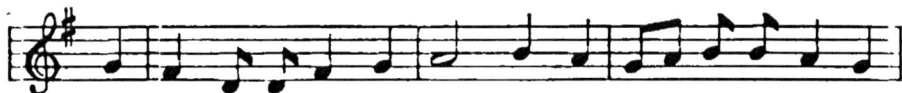

"And what did you see, my Ma - ry, All   up   on the Cal - don .

Low?   All   up   on   the Cal - don - Low?" "I

saw   the   blithe   sun - shine   come down, And   I

saw the mer - ry winds blow, And I saw the mer - ry winds blow."

HELPS TO STUDY

1. Who wandered up to the Caldon-Low and saw the fairies? 2. What did she tell her mother at first that she had seen? 3. How many fairies were there? 4. What music had they? 5. Who would be helped by the water? By the winds? By the scattering of the linseed? 6. Tell the story. 7. Can you sing the song, Caldon-Low?

LONGFELLOW

HENRY WADSWORTH LONGFELLOW

Henry Wadsworth Longfellow was a scholar, gentleman, and poet. We think of him as a poet, and of his poetry as that of a scholar and a gentleman.

He was born in Portland, Maine, in the same 5 year as Whittier, over a hundred years ago. He began school when he was three years old. His teachers were fond of him because he learned quickly and had a gentle disposition. While he was a little boy he loved the music of poetry so 10 well that he began to write verses himself. He went to Bowdoin College, where Hawthorne was his classmate. After getting all the education he could in his own country, he visited France, Italy, Spain, and afterwards Germany and other coun- 15 tries, so that he could learn what the older nations had to teach him. He kept on learning all his life, knew ten languages, and was for a long time Professor of Modern Languages at Harvard College. He did a great deal to 20 make Americans enjoy the books of other countries, partly by his teaching and partly by translating.

For the greater part of his life Longfellow lived
5 across the river from Boston, in Cambridge, in a house that had been Washington's headquarters. He had many friends. Strangers from every land came to see him. They were attracted by his winning manners as well as by his fame as a poet.
10 He not only knew the right and courteous way of doing everything, but he was also gentle in his thoughts and feelings. He was just as kind to a poor boy or an ignorant girl as to a great man or woman. He practiced the French saying *Noblesse*
15 *oblige,* which means that fortunate and happy people ought to be especially kind to those who are not so fortunate and happy. Longfellow put this beautiful feeling into his poems.

In his old age he came to be called "the chil-
20 dren's poet." This was partly because he loved children and partly because children loved him. In a poem called "The Children's Hour," he tells us about his three little daughters. In another

called "Children," he says that all his troubles go away when he sees children playing.

When Longfellow was grieved because a great chestnut tree in Cambridge was cut down, the children of the city brought their pennies to have 5 an arm-chair made out of the wood of the tree, and they gave the chair to him. He wrote a poem for them called "From My Arm-Chair," and he let every child who wanted to see the chair come to his house and sit in it. This was when 10 he was an old man, with silvery hair and beard. He died in 1882, at the age of seventy-five.

Longfellow wrote many poems that tell a story. *Hiawatha* is one. Another that you will wish to read some day is *Evangeline*. Perhaps you already 15 know his "Paul Revere's Ride." It is a short story of a stirring deed in Revolutionary times.

HIAWATHA'S FASTING

The stories in Longfellow's *Hiawatha* are the old Indian stories retold in verse. Hiawatha is the hero of the tribe, the man who has been bravest, wisest, and best. The stories tell how he did great things for his people: invented the bow and arrow, built the first canoe, and so on. This is their fanciful story of how he learned to grow corn, as a food for the winter to save his people from starving.

It is the custom in many savage tribes to make the young men bear a time of fasting, to test their strength and courage. It is at this time that Hiawatha wins for his people the victory over starvation.

On the fourth day of his fasting
In his lodge he lay exhausted;
From his couch of leaves and branches
Gazing with half-open eyelids,
5   Full of shadowy dreams and visions,
On the dizzy, swimming landscape,
On the gleaming of the water,
On the splendor of the sunset.

And he saw a youth approaching,
10   Dressed in garments green and yellow
Coming through the purple twilight,
Through the splendor of the sunset;

· Plumes of green bent o'er his forehead,
And his hair was soft and golden.

Standing at the open doorway,
Long he looked at Hiawatha,
Looked with pity and compassion   5
On his wasted form and features,
And, in accents like the sighing
Of the South-Wind in the tree-tops,
Said he, "O my Hiawatha!
All your prayers are heard in heaven,   10
For you pray not like the others;
Not for greater skill in hunting,
Not for greater craft in fishing,
Not for triumph in the battle,
Nor renown among the warriors,   15
But for profit of the people,
For advantage of the nations.

"From the Master of Life descending,
I, the friend of man, Mondamin,
Come to warn you and instruct you,   20
How by struggle and by labor
You shall gain what you have prayed for.
Rise up from your bed of branches,

Rise, O youth, and wrestle with me!"
Faint with famine, Hiawatha
Started from his bed of branches,
From the twilight of his wigwam
5 Forth into the flush of sunset
Came, and wrestled with Mondamin;
At his touch he felt new courage
Throbbing in his brain and bosom,
Felt new life and hope and vigor
10 Run through every nerve and fibre.

. . . .

On the morrow and the next day,
When the sun through heaven descending,
Like a red and burning cinder
From the hearth of the Great Spirit,
15 Fell into the western waters,
Came Mondamin for the trial,
For the strife with Hiawatha;
Came as silent as the dew comes,
From the empty air appearing,
20 Into empty air returning,
Taking shape when earth it touches,
But invisible to all men

In its coming and its going.
　Thrice they wrestled there together
In the glory of the sunset,
Till the darkness fell around them,
Till the heron, the Shuh-shuh-gah, 5
From her nest among the pine-trees,
Uttered her loud cry of famine,
And Mondamin paused to listen.
　Tall and beautiful he stood there,
In his garments green and yellow; 10
To and fro his plumes above him
Waved and nodded with his breathing,
And the sweat of the encounter
Stood like drops of dew upon him.
　And he cried, "O Hiawatha! 15
Bravely have you wrestled with me,
Thrice have wrestled stoutly with me,
And the Master of Life, who sees us,
He will give to you the triumph!"
　Then he smiled, and said: "To-morrow 20
Is the last day of your conflict,
Is the last day of your fasting.
You will conquer and o'ercome me:

Make a bed for me to lie in,
Where the rain may fall upon me,
Where the sun may come and warm me;
Strip these garments, green and yellow,
5 Strip this nodding plumage from me,
Lay me in the earth, and make it
Soft and loose and light above me.

  " Let no hand disturb my slumber,
Let no weed nor worm molest me,
10 Let not Kahgahgee, the raven,
Come to haunt me and molest me,
Only come yourself to watch me,
Till I wake, and start, and quicken,
Till I leap into the sunshine."

  · · · · · · ·

15 And behold! the young Mondamin,
With his soft and shining tresses,
With his garments green and yellow,
With his long and glossy plumage,
Stood and beckoned at the doorway.
20 And as one in slumber walking,
Pale and haggard, but undaunted,
From the wigwam Hiawatha

Came and wrestled with Mondamin.
    Round about him spun the landscape,
Sky and forest reeled together,
And his strong heart leaped within him,
As the sturgeon leaps and struggles   5
In a net to break its meshes.
Like a ring of fire around him
Blazed and flared the red horizon,
And a hundred suns seemed looking
At the combat of the wrestlers.   10
    Suddenly upon the greensward
All alone stood Hiawatha,
Panting with his wild exertion,
Palpitating with the struggle;
And before him breathless, lifeless,   15
Lay the youth, with hair dishevelled,
Plumage torn, and garments tattered,

    .   .   .   .

Dead he lay there in the sunset.
But the place was not forgotten
Where he wrestled with Mondamin;   20
Nor forgotten nor neglected
Was the grave where lay Mondamin,

    o

Sleeping in the rain and sunshine,
Where his scattered plumes and garments
Faded in the rain and sunshine.
    Day by day did Hiawatha
5 Go to wait and watch beside it;
Kept the dark mould soft above it,
Kept it clean from weeds and insects,
Drove away, with scoffs and shoutings,
Kahgahgee, the king of ravens.
10   Till at length a small green feather
From the earth shot slowly upward,
Then another and another,
And before the Summer ended
Stood the maize in all its beauty,
15 With its shining robes about it,
And its long, soft, yellow tresses;
And in rapture Hiawatha
Cried aloud, "It is Mondamin!
Yes, the friend of man, Mondamin!"

   .   .   .   .

20   And still later, when the Autumn
Changed the long, green leaves to yellow,
And the soft and juicy kernels

Grew like wampum hard and yellow,
Then the ripened ears he gathered,
Stripped the withered husks from off them,
As he once had stripped the wrestler,
Gave the first Feast of Mondamin,　　　5
And made known unto the people
This new gift of the Great Spirit.

HENRY WADSWORTH LONGFELLOW : *Hiawatha*

beckoned (bek'knd) : motioned to him to come

compassion (kom pash'un) : sorrow for the trouble of others

conflict (kon'flikt) : a fight

craft (kraft) : skill

dishevelled (di shev'ld) : in disorder

encounter (en koun'ter) : a struggle

exertion (egz er'shun) : effort

fasting (fast'ing) : going without food for a long time

flared (flârd) : gleamed, shone bright

haggard (hag'gard) : thin and weak

Hiawatha (Hē'ä wô'thä)

invisible (in viz'i bl) : not to be seen

maize (māz) : Indian corn

Mondamin (mon dä'min) : the Indian word for corn

palpitating (pal'pi tä'ting) : trembling

plumage (plūm'āj) : feathers, plumes

reeled (rēld) : spun round

renown (rē noun') : fame

sturgeon (stur'jŭn) : a large fish

triumph (tri'umph) : victory

twilight (twī'līt) : a half-light, like that between day and night

undaunted (un dônt'ed) : not afraid

wampum (wom'pum) : a small shell used as money by the Indians

HELPS TO STUDY

1. Hiawatha's "shadowy dreams and visions" come because he is weak from fasting. What figure comes to him? 2. What is it like? 3. How does it look like the

growing corn? 4. What trial of strength does Mondamin ask of Hiawatha? 5. How many wrestling matches do they have? 6. What does the spirit tell Hiawatha the end will be? 7. What is he to do then? 8. What does this mean? 9. How does Hiawatha carry out the orders? 10. What happens at the last? 11. What gift has Hiawatha won for his people? 12. What valuable things besides maize did people from Europe first find here in America?

REVIEW QUESTIONS

1. What does Caldon-Low mean? What things did the little girl in the poem see there? What good deeds were they doing?

2. What poems written by Longfellow can you name? Where was he born? Where did he travel and study? Where did he teach?

3. Who was Hiawatha? Why did he fast? What happened to him during his fasting? What good gift did he win for his people?

MAGGIE AND THE GYPSIES

Maggie Tulliver was a bright and kindly little girl, whose life was not always happy at home, because some of her family did not understand her. She had somehow got strange notions in her head about the wonderful life the gypsies led, and she thought she would be happy with them in their free and wandering life.

I

At the next bend in the lane Maggie saw the little black tent with the blue smoke rising before it, which was to be her refuge from all the unpleasant things in civilized life. She even saw a tall female figure by the column of smoke, 5 doubtless the gypsy mother, who provided the tea and other groceries.

"My little lady, where are you going to?" the gypsy said in a coaxing tone.

It was delightful, and just what Maggie expected; the gypsies saw at once that she was 5 a little lady, and were prepared to treat her so.

"Not any farther," said Maggie, feeling as if she were saying what she had rehearsed in a dream. "I'm come to stay with you, please."

"That's pretty; come, then. Why, what a 10 nice little lady you are, to be sure!" said the gypsy, taking her by the hand. Maggie thought her very agreeable, but wished she had not been so dirty.

There was quite a group round the fire when 15 they reached it. An old gypsy woman was seated on the ground nursing her knees, and occasionally poking a skewer into the round kettle, that sent forth an odorous steam; two small shock-headed children were lying prone and resting on 20 their elbows. A placid donkey was bending his head over a tall girl, who, lying on her back, was scratching his nose and indulging him with a bite of excellent stolen hay. The slanting sun-

light fell kindly upon them, and the scene was
really very pretty and comfortable, Maggie
thought, only she hoped they would soon set
out the tea cups.

At last the old woman said, —   5

"What! my pretty lady, are you come to stay
with us? Sit down and tell us where you live."

It was just like a story; Maggie liked to be
called pretty lady and treated in this way. She
sat down and said: 10

"I'm come from home because I'm unhappy, and I mean to be a gypsy. I'll live with you if you like, and teach you a great many things."

"Such a clever little lady," said the woman
5 with the baby, sitting down by Maggie, and allowing the baby to crawl, "and such a pretty bonnet and frock," she added, taking off Maggie's bonnet and looking at it while she made a remark to the old woman, in the unknown language.
10 The tall girl snatched the bonnet and, with a grin, put it on her own head hindforemost; but Maggie was determined not to show any weakness on this subject.

"I don't want to wear a bonnet," she said;
15 "I'd rather wear a red handkerchief, like yours" (looking at her friend by her side). "My hair was quite long till yesterday, when I cut it off, but I daresay it will grow again very soon," she added.

"Oh, what a nice little lady! — and rich, I'm
20 sure," said the old woman. "Didn't you live in a beautiful house at home?"

"Yes, my home is pretty, and I'm very fond of the river, where we go fishing, but I'm often very unhappy. I should have liked to bring my books with me, but I came away in a hurry, you know. But I can tell you almost everything there is in my books, I've read them so many times, and that will amuse you. And I can tell you something about geography too, — that's about the world we live in, — very useful and interesting. Did you ever hear about Columbus ? "

Maggie's eyes had begun to sparkle and her cheeks to flush, — she was really beginning to instruct the gypsies, and gaining great influence over them. The gypsies themselves were not without amazement at this talk, though their attention was divided by the contents of Maggie's pocket, which the friend at her right hand had by this time emptied without her knowing it.

"Is that where you live, my little lady ? " said the old woman, at the mention of Columbus.

"Oh, no ! " said Maggie, with some pity, " Columbus was a very wonderful man, who found out half the world, and they put chains on him and treated him very badly, you know; it's in my Catechism of Geography, but perhaps it's rather too long to tell before tea — I want my tea so."

The last words burst from Maggie, in spite of herself, with a sudden drop from fine talk to
5 simple peevishness.

"Why, she's hungry, poor little lady," said the younger woman. "Give her some o' the cold victual. You've been walking a good way, I'll be bound, my dear. Where's your home?"

10 "It's Dorlcote Mill, a good way off," said Maggie. "My father is Mr. Tulliver, but we mustn't let him know where I am, else he'll fetch me home again. Where does the queen of the gypsies live?"

15 "What! do you want to go to her, my little lady?" said the younger woman. The tall girl meanwhile kept staring at Maggie and grinning. Her manners were certainly not agreeable.

"No," said Maggie, "I'm only thinking that
20 if she isn't a very good queen you might be glad when she died, and you could choose another. If I was a queen, I'd be a very good queen, and kind to everybody."

"Here's a bit o' nice victual, then," said the old woman, handing to Maggie a lump of dry bread, which she had taken from a bag of scraps, and a piece of cold bacon.

"Thank you," said Maggie, looking at the food 5 without taking it, "but I'd like some bread and butter and tea instead. I don't like bacon."

"We've got no tea nor butter," said the old woman, with something like a scowl, as if she were getting tired of coaxing. 10

"Oh, a little bread and treacle would do," said Maggie.

"We han't got no treacle," said the old woman, crossly.

amazement (a māz'ment) : great surprise

catechism (kat'ē kizm) : a book presenting information in the form of questions and answers

civilized life (siv'i līzd līf) : the life of the people who live well and comfortably in good houses

han't got no treacle : What do you think of the gypsies' English ?

I'll be bound : I'm sure

indulging (in dulj'ing) : favoring

instruct (in strukt') : to teach

occasionally (ok ka'zhun al ly) : now and then

odorous (o'der us) : strong-smelling

placid (plas'id) : quiet, peaceful

prone (prōn) : flat on the ground

rehearsed (rē herst') : practised

scowl (skowl) : frown

shock-headed (shok'hed ed) : with hair thick and uncombed

skewer (skū'er) : a sharp-pointed iron rod

treacle (trēk'l) : sweet syrup

victual (vit'l) : food

II

Maggie felt very lonely, and was quite sure she should begin to cry before long; the gypsies didn't seem to mind her at all, and she felt quite weak among them. But the springing tears
5 were checked by new terror, when two men came up. The elder of the two carried a bag, which he flung down, addressing the women in a loud and scolding tone, which they answered by a shower of treble sauciness; while a black
10 cur ran barking up to Maggie, and threw her into a tremor that was made worse by the curses with which the younger man called the dog off, and gave him a rap with a great stick he held in his hand. At last the younger woman said,
15 "This nice little lady's come to live with us; aren't you glad?"

"Aye, very glad," said the younger man, who was looking at Maggie's silver thimble and other small matters that had been taken from her
20 pocket. He returned them all except the thimble to the younger woman, and she immediately restored them to Maggie's pocket.

Maggie began to think that Tom must be right about the gypsies; they must certainly be thieves, unless the man meant to return her thimble by and by.   She would willingly have given it to him, for she was not at âll attached to her 5 thimble.   The women saw she was frightened.

" We've got nothing nice, for a lady to eat," said the old woman in her coaxing tone.   " And she's so hungry, sweet little lady."

" Here, my dear, if you can eat a bit o' this," 10 said the younger woman, handing some of the stew on a brown dish with an iron spoon to Maggie, who, remembering that the old woman had seemed angry with her for not liking the bread and bacon, dared not refuse the stew, though 15 fear had chased away her appetite.   If her father would but come by in the gig and take her up! Or even if Jack the Giantkiller, or Mr. Greatheart, or St. George who slew the dragon on the half-pennies, would happen to pass that way!   But 20 Maggie thought with a sinking heart that these heroes were never seen about her home ; nothing very wonderful ever came there.

"What! you don't like the smell of it, my dear," said the young woman, observing that Maggie did not even take a spoonful of the stew. " Try a bit, come."

5 "No, thank you," said Maggie, summoning all her force for a desperate effort, and trying to smile in a friendly way. "I haven't time, I think; it seems getting darker. I think I must go home now, and come again another day, 10 and I can bring you a basket with some jam tarts and things."

Maggie rose from her seat, but her hope sank when the old gypsy woman said, "Stop a bit, stop a bit, little lady. We'll take you home, all safe, 15 when we've done supper; you shall ride home, like a lady."

Maggie sat down again, with little faith in this promise, though she presently saw the tall girl putting a bridle on the donkey, and throwing a 20 couple of bags on his back.

"Now, then, little missis," said the younger man, leading the donkey forward, "tell us where you live; what's the name o' the place?"

"Dorlcote Mill," said Maggie, eagerly. "My father is Mr. Tulliver; he lives there."

"What! a big mill this side o' St. Ogg's?"

"Yes," said Maggie. "Is it far off? I think I should like to walk there, if you please."   5

"It'll soon be getting dark; we must make haste. And the donkey'll carry you as nice as can be; you'll see."

He lifted Maggie as he spoke, and set her on the donkey. She felt relieved that it was not the old   10 man who seemed to be going with her, but she had only a trembling hope that she was really going home.

It now appeared that the man also was to be
5 seated on the donkey, holding Maggie before him. When the woman had patted her on the back and said "Good-by," the donkey, at a strong hint from the man's stick, set off at a rapid walk along the lane towards the point Maggie had come from
10 an hour ago, while the tall girl and the rough urchin, also furnished with sticks, obligingly escorted them for the first hundred yards, with much screaming and thwacking. As they reached a crossroad, Maggie caught sight of some one
15 coming on a white-faced horse.

"Oh, stop, stop!" she cried out. "There's my father! Oh, Father, Father!"

The sudden joy was almost painful, and before her father reached her, she was sobbing.
20 Great was Mr. Tulliver's wonder, for he had made a round from Basset, and had not yet been home.

"Why, what's the meaning o' this?" he said,

checking his horse, while Maggie slipped from the donkey and ran to her father's stirrup.

"The little miss lost herself, I reckon," said the gypsy. "She'd come to our tent at the far end o' Dunlow Lane, and I was bringing her where she said her home was. It's a good way to come arter being on the tramp all day."

"Oh, yes, Father, he's been very good to bring me home," said Maggie, — "a kind, good man!"

"Here, then, my man," said Mr. Tulliver, taking out five shillings. "It's the best day's work you ever did. I couldn't afford to lose the little girl; here, lift her up before me."

"Why, Maggie, how's this, how's this?" he said, as they rode along, while she laid her head against her father and sobbed. "How came you to be rambling about and lose yourself?"

"Oh, Father," sobbed Maggie, "I ran away because I was so unhappy; Tom was so angry with me. I couldn't bear it."

"Pooh, pooh," said Mr. Tulliver, soothingly, "you mustn't think o' running away from Father. What'ud Father do without his little girl?"

P

"Oh no, I never will again, Father — never."

Mr. Tulliver spoke his mind strongly at home that evening; and the effect was seen in the remarkable fact that Maggie never heard one re-
5 proach from her mother, or one taunt from Tom, about this foolish business of her running away to the gypsies. Maggie was rather impressed by this unusual treatment, and sometimes thought her conduct had been too wicked to be mentioned.

GEORGE ELIOT: *The Mill on the Floss* (ADAPTED).

arter (ar'ter): after
desperate (des'per ăt): strong
escorted (es kort'ed): went with
immediately (im mē'di ăt ly): at once
Mr. Greatheart (mist'er grāt'härt):
  a good man in Bunyan's *Pil-
  grim's Progress*, one of the books
  Maggie had read over and over

remarkable (rē mark' a bl): unusual
reproach (rē prōch'): blame
St. George (sănt jôrj): an imaginary
  English hero and saint
summoning: calling up
tremor (trē'môr): fright, fear
treble (treb'l): high-pitched, shrill
what'ud (whot''d): what would

HELPS TO STUDY

I. 1. How did Maggie like the gypsies? 2. What reason did she give for coming? 3. What things did they do that she didn't like so well? 4. How did she like their food?

II. 1. What made Maggie begin to feel afraid? 2. Tell about her starting for home and meeting her father. 3. What did she learn by her adventure? 4. Why was she not scolded for her running away?

COSETTE

The strong and kindly man in this story is Jean Valjean (pronounced Zhŏn Val′zhón) whose own life had been very unhappy, and who was still in hiding from the officers of the law.

I

It was Christmas Eve, and Cosette was in her usual place, seated on the crossbar of the kitchen table, near the fireplace. She was nearly eight years old, but she was so thin and pale that she seemed to be barely six. She was dressed in 5

227

rags; her bare feet were in wooden shoes; and by the light of the fire she was knitting woolen stockings for her mistress's little girls. In the next room could be heard the voices of the two 5 children laughing and prattling.

On this Christmas Eve several men were seated at the table in a low bare room of the Thénardiers' Inn. Four new travelers had just arrived. Cosette was thinking sadly that it was evening 10 and very dark, and that the pitchers in the rooms must be filled, and that there was no more water in the tank. From time to time one of the travelers would look out into the street and say, "It is as black as an oven outside!" or, "One would 15 have to be a cat to go along the streets to-night without a lantern," and Cosette trembled with fear.

Suddenly a man came in from the yard and said in a harsh voice, "My horse has not been 20 watered."

Cosette came out from under the table. "Oh, yes, sir!" she said, "the horse did have water. He drank a lot from the bucket. It was I who

carried the water to him and talked to him."
This was not true, but Cosette was afraid, so she
told a lie.

"Here is a girl as big as my fist who can tell a
lie as big as a house," said the man. "I say that
my horse has not had a bit of water."

Cosette crept back under the table, but Madame
Thénardier called angrily to her, "Come out of
there!" and when Cosette crawled out she said,
throwing open the door of the house, "Here, go,
and take some water to that horse."

"But Madame," said the child, timidly, "there
is no water."

"Go and get some, then, there is plenty in the
spring;" and as the landlady went back to the
stove she continued, "She is the laziest girl that
ever was." Then turning to Cosette she said:
"On the way back you are to get a loaf of bread
at the baker's. Here is the money."

Cosette went over to the fireplace for an empty
bucket that stood there. The bucket was so large
that she could have sat in it very easily. The
child had a small pocket in the side of her apron.

She took the money without saying a word, and dropped it into her pocket.   But she did not seem to see the open door.   "Get along with you!" cried Madame Thénardier.   Cosette went out, and ₅ the door closed behind her.

Just opposite the inn was a toyshop all gay with Christmas toys.   In the window was a large doll, nearly two feet high, dressed in a pink dress and with real hair and blue eyes.   Cosette called ₁₀ it "the lady."   All day this wonderful doll had stood there, for it seemed as if no mother was rich enough to buy it for her child.   As Cosette went out into the street, very miserable and frightened, she could not help looking over toward this won-₁₅ derful doll and saying to herself, "One would have to be a queen or at least a princess to have a doll like that!"   She was not able to turn her eyes away.   She forgot everything, even the errand on which she had been sent.   Suddenly ₂₀ she heard a harsh voice screaming, "Haven't you gone yet?   Be off with you!"   Cosette fled with her bucket, running as fast as she could.

The poor child now found herself alone in the

thick darkness. She rattled the handle of her
bucket so as to make some noise that would seem
to keep her company. She was not afraid as long
as the houses were in sight. Every now and then
she saw the light of a candle through the cracks 5
in a shutter, and this was a great comfort to her.
But when she had passed the last house she
stopped, for now all around her was the dark,
silent country. There were no people here, and
perhaps there were some wild beasts about. She 10
could almost hear them moving in the grass. "I
will go back," she said to herself.

Then she remembered Madame Thénardier's
cruel face and angry eyes. What was she to do?
What was to become of her? Where was she to 15
go? She took up the bucket again, and began to
run down the path toward the spring. She did
not turn her eyes to the right or the left for fear of
seeing things in the bushes.

crossbar: a wooden bar to hold the
legs of a table firmly together
would have to be a cat: that is,
have eyes like a cat's, that can see
in the dark

shutter: a wooden covering of a
window
Thénardier (Tā-nár-dē-ā)

II

The spring was a small natural basin about two feet deep, and paved with several large stones. Cosette did not take time to breathe. She bent down and plunged the bucket into the water. 5 She did not notice that something fell out of her pocket into the spring. She neither saw it nor heard it fall. She drew out the bucket nearly full, and set it on the grass. Then she sat down shivering. She had but one desire, which was to rush 10 through this fearful darkness to the houses, the windows, the lighted candles. But she dared not go without the bucket of water. She grasped the handle with both her hands, but she could hardly lift the bucket. She took a dozen steps, but the 15 bucket was so heavy that she was forced to set it on the ground. She took another breath, and lifted her load again. She walked bending forward, and with drooping head like an old woman. The iron handle was freezing her little wet hands. 20 The cold water splashed over her bare legs. She was in the depths of a forest at night, in winter,

far from human sight; and she was only eight
years old. Sobs choked her, but she did not dare
to cry, so afraid she was of her mistress even at
this distance.

Suddenly she was conscious that the weight of
the bucket was gone. A hand, which seemed to
her very large, had taken hold of the handle and
lifted it. Cosette raised her head. A large dark
figure was walking beside her. It was a man who
had come up behind her, though she had never
heard him. But she was not afraid. The man
spoke to her in a low voice. " My child," he said,
" this is very heavy for you."

" Yes, sir," said Cosette.

" Give it to me," said the stranger, " and I will
carry it for you."

Cosette let go of the handle, and the man
walked along beside her.

" How old are you, little one ? "

" Eight, sir."

" Are you going far with this ? "

" About a quarter of an hour's walk from
here."

The man said nothing for a moment, then he asked abruptly, "So you have no mother?"

"I don't know," answered the child. Then she added, "I don't think so. I don't know. Other ₅children have mothers."

"Where do you live, little one?"

"At the inn, if you know where that is."

"And who sent you at such an hour as this to get water in the forest?"

₁₀ "My mistress, Madame Thénardier," said Cosette.

"And what does your mistress do?" asked the man.

"She keeps the inn," replied the child.

₁₅ "The inn?" said the man. "Well, I am going to stay there to-night. Show me the way." In a little while the man said:

"Is there no servant in the inn?"

"No, sir."

₂₀ "Are you all alone there?"

"Yes, sir," replied Cosette. Then she added: "That is to say, there are two little girls."

"What little girls?"

"The landlady, Madame Thénardier's."

"And what do these little girls do?"

"Oh," said the child. "They have beautiful dolls, and they play all day long."

"And you?" 5

"I? Oh, I work."

"All day long?"

The child raised her face and said gently, "Yes, sir." After a silence she continued, "Sometimes, when I have finished my work, they let me play, 10 but I have only a lead sword to play with. It is about as big as that," and she held up her tiny finger. As they came near the inn, Cosette said timidly, "Will you let me take the bucket now, for if Madame sees that some one has carried it 15 for me she will beat me?"

The man gave her the bucket, and in a moment they were at the door of the inn. Cosette knocked, and the landlady appeared with a candle in her hand. "So it's you, is it?" she cried angrily. 20 "You seem to have taken your time."

"Madame," said Cosette trembling, "Here is a gentleman who wants a lodging."

COSETTE AND HER BIG FRIEND.

"Come in, sir," said the landlady; and the man entered, and he seated himself at the table. Cosette took up her old place under the kitchen table and went on with her knitting. Wet and cold as she was, she did not dare to go near the fire. Suddenly Madame exclaimed: "Where's that bread?" Cosette thrust her hand into her pocket, and then turned white. The money was not there. "Have you lost it?" screamed the landlady, reaching out her hand toward a whip that hung on the wall. The man had been watching Cosette. "Here, Madame," he said. "Here is the money. It fell from the little girl's pocket."

"Yes, that is it," said the landlady. It was much more than she had given Cosette, but she put it in her pocket, and threw an ugly look at the child.

"What is she knitting?" the man asked in a gentle voice.

"Stockings, if you please," said Madame. "Stockings for my little girls." The man looked at Cosette's poor little red feet. "When will she finish this pair of stockings?" he asked.

"It will take her three or four days yet, the lazy thing," said Madame.

"And how much will the stockings be worth when they are done?"

5 The landlady looked at him. "Five francs, at least."

"Will you take that for them now?" asked the man. The innkeeper thought it was time for him to speak.

10 "Yes," he said, "you may have them for five francs. We can refuse nothing to travelers."

"You must pay for them now," said Madame sharply.

"I will buy that pair of stockings," said the 15 man, drawing the money from his pocket and laying it on the table. Then he turned to Cosette. "Now your work belongs to me; you need not finish the stockings; you may play, my child."

"Is it true, Madame? May I play?"

20 "Play!" said the landlady in a terrible voice.

"Thank you, Madame," said Cosette, and while her mouth spoke these thanks, her whole little soul thanked the traveler.

III

Meantime the landlady's little girls had been playing with their doll, and had left it on the floor while they dressed up a kitten. Cosette now fixed up her little lead sword for a doll, and rocking it in her arms, she pretended to put it to sleep. 5 Suddenly she paused and turned around, for she had caught sight of the doll which the landlady's children had left on the floor near the kitchen table. Cosette dropped the lead sword, and crept out from under the table on her hands and knees. 10 She seized the doll, and in a moment was back in her place again.

This joy lasted about a quarter of an hour. Then Cosette let one of the doll's legs stick out so that the firelight shone on it. This caught the 15 landlady's eye. "Cosette!" she screamed, in a terrible voice. Cosette started as if the ground were trembling beneath her. She laid the doll gently on the floor, then wringing her hands she burst into tears. 20

The traveler rose to his feet. "What is the matter?" he asked.

"Don't you see?" cried Madame. "She has dared to touch the children's doll."

"Well, what of it?" said the man.

"She touched it with her dirty hands, with her 5 disgusting hands," almost screamed the landlady.

The man walked straight to the street door, opened it, and went out. Soon the door opened again, and in came the man carrying in his hands the beautiful doll of the toyshop. He walked 10 over to Cosette, and placing the doll in front of her said, "This is for you." Cosette raised her eyes, and gazed at the man as she might have gazed at the sun coming near her. She stared at the man, then at the doll. Then she slowly 15 crawled under the table and hid herself as far away as she could.

"Well, Cosette," said the landlady, in a voice that she tried to make sweet. "Aren't you going to take your doll? The gentleman has given it 20 to you."

Cosette gazed at the wonderful doll. Her face was wet with tears, but her smile was beautiful. She felt as if some one had said to her:

"Little one, you are the Queen of France."

She went up timidly to the landlady. "May I really have it?" she asked.

"It is yours. The gentleman has given it to you," said Madame.

"Is it true, sir? Is it really true?" cried Cosette. "Is 'the lady' mine?"

The stranger's eyes filled with tears. He nodded to Cosette, and placed "the lady's" tiny

Q

hand in hers.   In a moment Cosette held the ribbons and fresh pink dress of the doll against her own rags.   "I shall call her Catherine," she said. So Cosette went off to bed carrying Catherine in
5 her arms.

Some time later, when the house was still and every one was asleep, the stranger passed through the rooms as if looking for something.   Under the staircase, amidst all sorts of dust and rubbish and
10 spiders' webs, there was a bed — if it could be called a bed.   It was an old straw mattress full of holes, and on it were neither pillows nor sheets. In this bed, Cosette was sleeping.   She was sleeping soundly, all dressed; and clasped tight in her
15 arms was the doll, whose wide blue eyes shone in the darkness.

VICTOR HUGO: *Les Miserables* (ADAPTED).

HELPS TO STUDY

1. In what way does this story remind you of Cinderella? 2. Tell the story aloud after you have read it through. 3. What day of the year was it? 4. This story is taken from a famous French book, *Les Miserables* (Lā Mē'zer ä'bl), which means the unhappy, or the unfortunate.

HEIDI'S FIRST DAY ON THE MOUNTAIN

Heidi is a little Swiss girl, whose father and mother are dead. She is brought to her old grandfather who is living alone up on the side of one of the mountains of the Alps. She has never been up on the mountains before, and the beauty of them is all new and wonderful to her. You will enjoy reading, some time, the whole book from which this story is taken. Heidi has been sleeping on the soft hay in the loft, and her first day in the mountains now begins.

I

Early the next morning Heidi was awakened by a shrill whistle, and on opening her eyes saw the yellow sunlight shining through the loophole, full on her bed and on the hay beside it, turning it all to shimmering gold. Heidi looked about5 her in surprise, and wondered where she was.

But soon she heard her grandfather's deep voice outside, and then it all came back to her — where she had come from, and that now she was to live with him up on the Alm. And so Heidi was very10 glad when she awoke in her new home and thought of everything — all the new things she had seen yesterday, and what she would see again to-day.

So she jumped quickly out of bed and was soon dressed. Then she climbed down the ladder and ran out through the open door. There stood Peter with his goats, and her grandfather was just opening the stable door to let Swanli and Bearli out to join the others. Heidi ran toward the old man to say good-morning to him and the goats.

"Would you like to go with them up to the pasture?" he asked. There was nothing that Heidi would have liked better, and she danced up and down for joy at the very thought.

"But first you must wash yourself and be tidy, else the sun that is always so shiny and bright up yonder, will laugh to see you look so black. See, everything is ready for you over there," said her grandfather, as he pointed to a large tub full of water standing in the sunshine before the door.

Heidi ran to it and splashed and rubbed until she was so clean that she shone. Meanwhile her grandfather went into the hut and called to Peter:

"Come here, commander of goats, and bring your haversack with you."

In great surprise, Peter followed him into the house and held out the little bag in which he carried his meager dinner.

"Open it," was the old man's next order; then he put into it a huge slice of bread and an equally large piece of cheese. Peter looked on in round-eyed wonder, for the two pieces were each half again as large as those which had been put in for his dinner.

"There; now the bowl must go in," said the grandfather. "You are to fill the bowl twice for her dinner, for she is going with you and will stay until you come back. Take good care of her, and don't let her fall over the cliffs, do you hear?"

Heidi now came running up.

"Will the sun find anything to laugh at now, Grandfather?" she asked anxiously. In her fear of the sun's laughter she had rubbed her face, neck, and arms so vigorously with the coarse towel that her grandfather had hung beside the tub, that she now stood before him as red as a lobster. The old man smiled as he looked at her.

"No, he'll find nothing to laugh at now. But I will tell you something; this evening, when you 5 get home, you must jump into the water all over, just like a fish, for little folks that run about with the goats get black feet just like them. Now you can all be off."

Away they went, up the mountain, as merry as 10 could be. The wind that had blown so hard all night had not left a cloud in the sky. From the deep blue overhead, the glorious sun poured its warmth and light down on the mountain side until all the blue and yellow flowers opened wide 15 their cups and smiled back at it in gratitude. Heidi ran hither and thither, shouting for joy; for here were whole troops of delicate, pink primroses, and beyond them the ground was blue with gentians, while everywhere were nodding yellow 20 rockroses dancing in the golden sunshine. So delighted was Heidi with all these nodding and shining blossoms that she quite forgot the goats, and even Peter himself. She ran far ahead, and

then off to one side, for here she saw a sheen of
red, and yonder a glimmer of yellow which she
could not resist. And wherever she went she
gathered great bunches of the gay blossoms and

stowed them away in her apron, for she meant to 5
take them home with her and set them all round
in the hay up in her loft so that her sleeping room
might be as beautiful as it was here.

" You have enough flowers now," said Peter as
the two were again clambering upward together; 10

" else you'll be stopping all along the way. And besides, if you take them all to-day, there'll be none left for to-morrow."

The last reason appealed to Heidi. Moreover, her apron was already so full of flowers there was little room for more, and to-morrow she would come again to see them. So she trudged along at Peter's side; and the goats, too, were more tractable, for they sniffed from afar the tempting fragrance of the herbs that awaited them on the upper pastures, and so climbed on without delay.

Alm (alm) : an open meadow high up on the mountain side

delicate (del'i căt) : fine and dainty

gratitude (grat i tūd) : thankfulness

haversack (hav'er sak) : a small pack carried on the back

Heidi (hī'di)

meager (mē'ger) : small

sheen (shēn) : a bright light

shimmering (shim'er ing) : shining and quivering

tractable (tract'a bl) : obedient, easily managed

vigorously (vig'er us lў) : hard, strongly

II

The grazing place where Peter usually made a halt with his goats, and set up his quarters for the day, lay at the foot of great cliffs whose base was green with bushes and scrub pines, but whose jagged peaks towered bare and bleak into the heavens.

On one side the pasture lands fell away in sheer precipices to the valley below, and grandfather's warning with regard to them was not without reason.

Heidi looked so long and steadily at the high 5 mountain peaks, that at length they seemed all to have faces and to be looking back at her like good old friends.

Suddenly she heard loud, shrill cries above her in the air, and looking up beheld the largest bird 10

she had ever seen, poised above her on wide out-
stretched wings; then it soared about in great
circles, returning again and again to a point just
over her head.

5 "Peter, Peter, wake up!" cried Heidi as loud
as she could. "See, the eagle has come! See,
there, there!"

Peter roused himself at her cry of alarm, and the
two children watched the bird as it rose higher and
10 higher into the blue dome above and finally vanished behind the gray cliffs.

"Where has he gone?" asked Heidi, whose eyes
had followed the bird with the deepest interest.

"Home, to his nest," was Peter's answer.

15 "Is his home away up yonder? Oh, how
lovely to live so high up. Why does he scream
so?" Heidi continued her questioning.

"Because he must," was Peter's explanation.

"Let us climb up there and see where he lives,"
20 proposed Heidi.

"Oh! Oh! Oh!" Peter broke forth, each
exclamation marked by a tone of greater dis-
approval. "Why, even the goats can't get up

there, and your grandfather said you were not to fall over the cliffs."

And now Peter set up such a tremendous shouting and whistling that Heidi wondered what was going to happen. But the goats must have understood it well enough, for they came jumping and running down the mountain side, one after the other, until the whole flock was assembled on the green pasture, some nibbling away at the juicy stalks, others skipping hither and thither, while still others tried their horns on one another in playful combat.

Heidi had jumped to her feet and was soon in the midst of them, for to her it was a new and highly amusing sight to see the little creatures skip about and carry on their merry antics. She ran from one to the other, getting personally acquainted with each in turn, for no two were alike; each had its own peculiar appearance and ways.

Thus the day slipped by unnoticed, and already the sun was nearing the tops of the western mountains. Heidi was sitting very quietly on the ground looking at the bluebells and tender rock-roses glistening in the golden evening sunshine; even the grass had caught the golden light, and the cliffs above were beginning to gleam and glow, ⁵when suddenly the child sprang to her feet, crying:

"Peter! See! The fire, the fire, Peter! All the mountains are in flames, and the big snow field yonder is burning, and the sky! Oh, look, look! The great rocks are all red! Oh, the ¹⁰beautiful burning snow! Peter, get up! See, the fire has reached the eagle's nest! Oh, do look at the rocks! Look at the pine trees! Everything, everything is on fire!"

"It is always so," said Peter quite unmoved as ¹⁵he whittled away at his stick, "but it's no fire."

"What is it, then?" asked Heidi eagerly, and ran hither and thither to look in every direction, for she could not see enough, it was so beautiful on every side.

²⁰ "What is it, Peter? What is it?" she asked again.

"Oh, it just comes so of itself," was Peter's explanation.

"Oh, see, see!" cried Heidi in great excitement, "all the mountains are turning rosy-red! Look at the one with the snow, and that one with the high, pointed cliffs! What are their names, Peter? What are their names?" 5

"Mountains have no names," was the reply.

"Oh, how beautiful! Look at the pink snow! And oh, see all the many, many roses up yonder on the rocks! Oh, now they are turning gray! Oh, oh! Now it is all fading out! Now it is all 10 gone, Peter!" And Heidi sat down on the grass looking as sad as though the world were coming to an end.

"To-morrow it will be so again," said Peter. "Come, get up; we must go home now." 15

The boy shouted and whistled for his goats, and then the whole company started homeward.

"Will it be so every day, every day that we come up here?" asked Heidi, in eager hope of an assuring answer as she trudged along at Peter's side. 20

"Usually," was the answer.

"But to-morrow? Are you sure it will be so to-morrow?" she wanted to know.

"Yes, yes; to-morrow, of course!" Peter assured her, whereupon Heidi's good spirits returned.

But she had seen so much that was new, and ₅had so many things to think about, that she was quite silent all the way down to her grandfather's cottage.

JOHANNA SPYRI: *Heidi* (ADAPTED).

antics (an'tiks): tricks, play

precipices (pres'i pis): high, steep rocks

sheer (shēr): steep and straight

tremendous (trē men'dus): very great

vanished (van'ish'd): disappeared

HELPS TO STUDY

I. 1. How is Heidi's day to be spent? 2. Who is to be her guide? 3. What does her grandfather tell her about being clean? 4. What flowers does she see?

II. 1. What great bird flies above them? 2. What was the most wonderful sight of the whole day? What caused it? The common name for it in Switzerland is "the Alpen-glow." 3. How did Peter call his goats together? 4. What do you think of the way Peter explains things?

HEIDI'S RETURN TO THE MOUNTAIN

In the last story, we read how Heidi loved her new home in the mountains. After she had been there a while, she went to a rich home in the city of Frankfort to be a companion to a crippled girl. But she grew ill from homesickness; she could not sleep well, and began to walk in her sleep. When her kind employers found out what was the matter, they sent her back to her mountain home.

I

Heidi bade her friend "Good-night," and, with her basket on her arm, began to climb up toward the Alm. The green mountain slope was bright with the rays of the setting sun, and soon the great snow field on Casaplana came in view, glit-5 tering in the sunlight. After every few steps Heidi stood still and looked backward, for as she climbed up, the high mountains lay behind her. Suddenly the grass at her feet became tinged with red; she turned—and lo! a splendor such as 10 neither her memory nor her dreams had ever painted. The jagged peaks of Falkniss flamed red against the sky, the great snow field was aglow, while rosy clouds drifted across it. The grass on

HEIDI COMES HOME AGAIN.

the mountain side had turned to gold, every cliff shimmered and shone, and, far below, the valley lay afloat in a sea of golden mist.

Heidi stood in the midst of all this splendor, and so great was her happiness and joy that the tears rolled down her cheeks as she folded her hands and looked up to heaven to thank the dear God for bringing her back to her home again. Everything was so beautiful, so much more beautiful than she had thought, and now it was all hers once more. And the child felt so glad, and so rich in this wealth of beauty about her, that she could not find words in which to express her gratitude to the dear God in Heaven. Not until the light began to fade could she move from the spot; but then she ran so quickly up the mountain that it was not long before she saw the tops of the pine trees above the roof, and at last the cottage itself with her grandfather sitting on the bench in front of it smoking his pipe, while above it the old pine trees swayed and sighed in the evening breeze. Now Heidi ran faster than ever, and before the Alm-Uncle knew what it was that was coming up

R

the mountain so fast, the child was at his side. Dropping her basket on the ground she threw her arms around the old man's neck and cried:

"Grandfather, Grandfather, Grandfather!" for this was all she could say in the joy of seeing him again.

The old man also had nothing to say. For the first time in many years his eyes were wet with tears and he had to dry them with the back of his hand. Then he unclasped Heidi's arms from about his neck and set the child upon his knee. After looking down at her a moment, he said:

"So you have come home, Heidi; how did that happen? Very proud you do not look. Did they send you away?"

"Oh, no, Grandfather, you must not think that," Heidi began very earnestly. "They were all very good to me, Klara and the grandmamma and Herr Sesemann. But you see, Grandfather, I could hardly stand it until I could get home again to you, and sometimes it seemed to me I could not breathe for the lump in my throat. But I did not say anything, for that would have been ungrateful.

Then all at once Herr Seseman sent for me early one morning.   I think the Herr Doctor had something to do with that — but perhaps the letter tells all about it."   With these words Heidi jumped to her feet, and quickly took the letter and package out of her basket and laid them in her grandfather's hand.

"That belongs to you," said he, laying the package on the bench beside her.   Then he read the letter, and without a word, put it into his pocket.

"Do you think you could drink some milk with me, Heidi?" he asked as he took the child by the hand and went toward the door of the hut.   "But take your money with you, Heidi; it will buy a bed and bedding, and clothes enough to last you a couple of years."

"Indeed, I do not need it, Grandfather," Heidi assured him, "for I have a bed, and Klara packed so many clothes into my trunk that I shall never need any more."

"Take it, take it, child, and put it away in the closet; some day you will find a use for it."

Heidi obeyed and, hopping and skipping, followed her grandfather into the house. Here she ran from one corner to another in the joy of greeting all the old familiar things. Then she climbed
5 up the ladder to the loft, but came to a sudden stop, and cried down in great alarm:

"Oh, Grandfather, my bed is gone!"

"It will soon be back," came the answer from below. "I did not know that you were coming
10 home. Now come down and get some milk."

Heidi ran down and, fetching her high chair, seated herself in her accustomed place. Taking up her little bowl she set it to her lips and drank eagerly, as though she had never had anything so
15 good in all her life before. When she had drained it, she set it down, and drawing a deep breath, said:

"There is nothing in the world as good as our milk, Grandfather!"

accustomed (ak kus'tumd): usual
Casaplana (Käz'ä plä'nä)
Falkniss (Fôlk'nis)

gratitude (grat'ĭ tūd): thankfulness
jagged (jăg'gd): rough and broken
Sesemann (Sā'zä mon)

II

Suddenly a shrill whistle was heard without;
like a flash Heidi was out of the door.   There,
from the heights above, came the whole flock of
goats, skipping, jumping, leaping into the air,
and Goat-Peter in their midst.   When he saw 5
Heidi he stood as though rooted to the ground,
and stared at her in speechless amazement.   Heidi
called out: " Good evening, Peter! " and rushed
in among the goats, crying :

" Swanli! Bearli! It is I! Don't you know me ? " 10

The little creatures must have recognized her
voice, for instantly they began to bleat in an agitated manner, and Heidi called them all by name
as they ran frantically about and pushed one
another in their joy and eagerness to get near her. 15
That impatient fellow, Goldfinch, took a leap over
two of the other goats, so as to get close to her,
and even timid little Snowhopli wedged her way
through most persistently, even pushing aside the
big Turk who looked amazed at such impudence, 20
and raised his bearded chin high in air to show
that it was he who was being thus treated.

Heidi was almost beside herself with joy at seeing all her old playfellows once more; again and again she threw her arms around delicate Snow-hopli's neck and stroked the glossy coat of bois-
5 terous Goldfinch, never heeding the familiar way in which she was being pushed from side to side by the goats in their eagerness, until she found herself close beside Peter who had not moved from the spot.

10 "Come down, Peter, and say 'Good-evening,'" Heidi called to him.

"So you have come back, have you?" the boy's surprise at length allowed him to say, as he came nearer and took Heidi's hand, which she had been
15 holding out to him for some time. Then he asked as he always had when parting from Heidi after a day spent up on the pasture:

"Are you coming with us again to-morrow?"

"Not to-morrow, but the day after, perhaps.
20 To-morrow I must go to the grandmother's."

"It is good to see you back again," said Peter, drawing his face into wonderful wrinkles of delight; then he turned homeward. But he found his goats more unmanageable than ever before, for, when with coaxing and driving he had at length succeeded in gathering them all around himself, they suddenly turned about and all ran after Heidi who was walking off with one[5] arm around Bearli's neck and the other around Swanli's. Heidi had to go into the stable with her goats, and close the door after her, else Peter would never have got off with his flock at all.

[10]

When the child returned to the hut she found her bed all ready for her. The fragrant hay, only recently mowed, was piled high, and over it the grandfather had carefully spread the clean sheet and coverlet. It was a great joy to Heidi to climb[15] into it, and she slept more soundly than she had for over a year.

During the night her grandfather left his bed no less than ten times, and softly mounting the ladder, listened to assure himself that Heidi was[20] asleep and not tossing restlessly. Then he would feel for the round loophole to learn whether the hay with which he had carefully closed it was still firmly in place; for henceforth the moon must not be allowed to shine on Heidi's couch.

But the child slept on without once waking, and did not stir from her bed, for now her great and 5 burning desire was fulfilled: she had seen all the peaks and cliffs bathed in the sunset glow; she had heard the old pine trees sigh in the evening wind; she was at home again.

JOHANNA SPYRI: *Heidi* (ADAPTED).

agitated (aj′i tāt′ed): excited
frantically (fran′ti kal lỹ): wildly
fragrant (frā′grant): sweet-smelling

fulfilled (ful fild′): satisfied
recognized (rek′og nīz d): known

HELPS TO STUDY

I. 1. What did Heidi see as she climbed up to the cottage? 2. Tell about the meeting between her and her grandfather. 3. What do you think was in the letter Heidi brought? 4. What did she want to do with her money?

II. 1. How did the goats welcome Heidi? 2. What did Peter say? 3. How did his face show his delight? 4. Why did the grandfather go to look at Heidi so often during the night? 5. Had the letter anything to do with his watching Heidi? 6. Why did he not let the moon shine on her couch? 7. Have you ever been homesick? 8. Tell about the most beautiful place you have ever seen.

THE VILLAGE BLACKSMITH

Under a spreading chestnut-tree
   The village smithy stands;
The smith, a mighty man is he,
   With large and sinewy hands;
And the muscles of his brawny arms   5
   Are strong as iron bands.

His hair is crisp, and black, and long;
   His face is like the tan;
His brow is wet with honest sweat,
   He earns whate'er he can,
5 And looks the whole world in the face,
   For he owes not any man.

Week in, week out, from morn till night,
   You can hear his bellows blow;
You can hear him swing his heavy sledge,
10   With measured beat and slow,
Like a sexton ringing the village bell,
   When the evening sun is low.

And children coming home from school
   Look in at the open door;
15 They love to see the flaming forge,
   And hear the bellows roar,
And catch the burning sparks that fly
   Like chaff from a threshing-floor.

He goes on Sunday to the church,
20   And sits among his boys;
He hears the parson pray and preach,

He hears his daughter's voice
Singing in the village choir,
   And it makes his heart rejoice.

It sounds to him like her mother's voice
   Singing in Paradise!   5
He needs must think of her once more,
   How in the grave she lies;
And with his hard, rough hand he wipes
   A tear out of his eyes.

Toiling, — rejoicing, — sorrowing,   10
   Onward through life he goes;
Each morning sees some task begin,
   Each evening sees it close;
Something attempted, something done,
   Has earned a night's repose.   15

Thanks, thanks to thee, my worthy friend,
   For the lesson thou hast taught!
Thus at the flaming forge of life
   Our fortunes must be wrought;
Thus on its sounding anvil shaped   20
   Each burning deed and thought.

                        HENRY W. LONGFELLOW.

repose (rē pōz') : rest
sinewy and brawny (sin ū ȳ, braun'ȳ):
    strong and muscular

smithy (smith'y) : blacksmith's shop
threshing-floor (thresh'ing flōr) : a
    floor for beating out grain

HELPS TO STUDY

1. Where is the smithy? 2. How does the smith look? What things in him do we admire? 3. Why can he "look the whole world in the face"? 4. Why do the children stop at the smithy? 5. What does the smith think of at church? 6. We often hear the phrase, "the dignity of labor"; how does it fit this man? 7. What lessons should we learn from him? 8. Tell about a visit of your own to some workshop.

REVIEW QUESTIONS

1. Why did Maggie Tulliver run away from home? Why did she go to the gypsies? What did she hope to become among them? What did she want to teach them? What kind of people did she find they really were?

2. Who was Cosette? How was she treated? What kind friend did she find? Where? What did he do for her?

3. Tell where Heidi lived. What did she see on her first day in the mountains? What was the finest sight of all? How did she show her joy at getting back to the mountains? How did Peter show his pleasure?

4. What sort of man was the village blacksmith? Of what did his daughter's singing remind him?

JACKANAPES AND THE PONY

"The Green" proper was originally only part of a straggling common, which in its turn merged into some wilder waste land where Gypsies sometimes squatted if the authorities would allow them, especially after the annual Fair. And it was after the Fair that Jackanapes, out rambling by himself, was knocked over by the Gypsy's son riding the Gypsy's red-haired pony at break-neck pace across the common.

Jackanapes got up and shook himself, none the worse, except for being heels over head in love with the red-haired pony. What a rate he went at! How he spurned the ground with his nimble feet! How his red coat shone in the sunshine! And what bright eyes peeped out of his dark fore-lock as it was blown by the wind!

The Gypsy boy had had a fright, and he was willing enough to reward Jackanapes for not hav-ing been hurt, by consenting to let him have a ride.

"Do you mean to kill the little fine gentleman, and swing us all on the gibbet, you rascal?" screamed the Gypsy-mother, who came up just as Jackanapes and the pony set off.

"He would get on," replied her son. "It'll not kill him. He'll fall on his yellow head, and it's as tough as a cocoanut."

But Jackanapes did not fall. He stuck to the red-haired pony as he had stuck to the hobby-horse; but oh, how different the delight of this wild gallop with flesh and blood! Just as his legs were beginning to feel as if he did not feel them, the Gypsy boy cried "Lollo!" Round went the pony so unceremoniously, that, with as little ceremony, Jackanapes clung to his neck, and he 5 did not properly recover himself before Lollo stopped with a jerk at the place where they had started.

"Is his name Lollo?" asked Jackanapes, his hand lingering in the wiry mane.   10

"Yes."

"What does Lollo mean?"

"Red."

"Is Lollo your pony?"

"No. My father's." And the Gypsy boy led 15 Lollo away.

At the first opportunity Jackanapes stole away again to the common. This time he saw the Gypsy-father, smoking a dirty pipe.

"Lollo is your pony, isn't he?" said Jacka- 20 napes.

"Yes."

"He's a very nice one."

"He's a racer."

"You don't want to sell him, do you?"

"Fifteen pounds," said the Gypsy-father; and Jackanapes sighed and went home again. That very afternoon he and Tony rode the two donkeys, and Tony managed to get thrown, and even Jackanapes' donkey kicked. But it was jolting, clumsy work after the elastic swiftness and the dainty mischief of the red-haired pony.

A few days later Miss Jessamine spoke very seriously to Jackanapes. She was a good deal agitated as she told him that his grandfather the General was coming to the Green, and that he must be on his very best behavior during the visit. If it had been feasible to leave off calling him Jackanapes and to get used to his baptismal name of Theodore before the day after to-morrow (when the General was due), it would have been satisfactory. But Miss Jessamine feared it would be impossible in practice, and she had scruples about it on principle. It would not seem quite truthful, although she had always most fully intended that he should be called Theodore when he had outgrown the ridiculous appropriateness of his nickname.   The fact was that he had not out-grown it, but he must take care to remember who was meant when his grandfather said Theodore.

Indeed for that matter he must take care all 5 along.

"You are apt to be giddy, Jackanapes," said Miss Jessamine.

"Yes, aunt," said Jackanapes, thinking of the hobbyhorses.   10

"You are a good boy, Jackanapes.   I am glad I can tell your grandfather that;   an obe-dient boy, an honorable boy, and a kind-hearted boy.   But you are — in short, you are a Boy, Jackanapes.   And I hope " — added Miss Jessa- 15 mine, desperate with the results of experience — " that the General knows that boys will be boys."

What mischief could be foreseen Jackanapes promised to guard against.   He was to keep his clothes and his hands clean, to look over his cate- 20 chism, not to put sticky things in his pockets, to keep that hair of his smooth — (" It's the wind that blows it, Aunty," said Jackanapes — " I'll

s

send by the coach for some bear's grease," said
Miss Jessamine, tying a knot in her pocket handkerchief) — not to burst in at the parlor door, not
to talk at the top of his voice, not to crumple his
5 Sunday frill, and to sit quite quiet during the ser-
mon, to be sure to say "sir" to the General, to be
careful about rubbing his shoes on the door mat,
and to bring his lesson books to his aunt at once
that she might iron down the dogs' ears.   The
10 General arrived, and for the first day all went well,
except that Jackanapes' hair was as wild as usual,
for the hairdresser had no bear's grease left.   He
began to feel more at ease with his grandfather,
and disposed to talk confidentially with him, as he
15 did with the Postman.   All that the General felt
it would take too long to tell, but the result was
the same.   He was disposed to talk confidentially
with Jackanapes.

"Very pretty place, this," he said, looking out
20 of the lattice on to the Green, where the grass
was vivid with sunset, and the shadows were long
and peaceful.

"You should see it in Fair-week, sir," said Jack-

anapes, shaking his yellow mop, and leaning back
in one of the two Chippendale armchairs in which
they sat.

"A fine time that, eh?" said the General, with
a twinkle in his left eye. (The other was glass.) 5

Jackanapes shook his hair once more. "I enjoyed this last one the best of all," he said. "I
had so much money."

"Well, well, it's not a common complaint in
these bad times. How much had you?" 10

"I had two shillings: a new shilling Aunty gave
me, and elevenpence I had saved up, and a penny
from the Postman — sir!" added Jackanapes with
a jerk, having forgotten it.

"And how did you spend it — sir?" inquired the 15
General.

Jackanapes spread his ten fingers on the arms
of his chair, and shut his eyes that he might count
the more conscientiously.

"Watch stand for Aunty, threepence. Trumpet 20
for myself, twopence, that's fivepence. Ginger
nuts for Tony, twopence, and a mug with a
grenadier on for the Postman, fourpence, that's

elevenpence.   Shooting gallery, a penny, that's a
shilling.   Giddy-go-round, a penny, that's one and
a penny.   Treating Tony, one and twopence.
Flying Boats (Tony paid for himself), a penny,
5 one and threepence.   Shooting gallery again, one
and fourpence.   Fat Woman, a penny, one and
fivepence.   Giddy-go-round again, one and six-
pence. Shooting gallery, one and sevenpence.
Treating Tony, and then he wouldn't shoot, so I
10 did, one and eightpence.   Living skeleton, a penny
—no, Tony treated me, the Living Skeleton
doesn't count.   Skittles, a penny, one and nine-
pence.   Mermaid (but when we got inside she was
dead), a penny, one and tenpence.   Theater, a
15 penny (Priscilla Partington, or the Green Lane
Murder.   A beautiful young lady, sir, with pink
cheeks and a real pistol), that's one and elevenpence.   Ginger beer, a penny (I was so thirsty!),
two shillings.   And then the shooting gallery
20 man gave me a turn for nothing, because, he said,
I was a real gentleman, and spent my money like
a man."

"So you do, sir, so you do!" cried the General.

"Why, sir, you spend it like a prince. And now I suppose you've not got a penny in your pocket?"

"Yes, I have," said Jackanapes. "Two pennies. They are saving up." And Jackanapes jingled them with his hand.

"You don't want money except at Fair-times, I suppose?" said the General.

Jackanapes shook his mop.

"If I could have as much as I want, I should know what to buy," said he.

"And how much do you want, if you could get it?"

"Wait a minute, sir, till I think what twopence from fifteen pounds leaves. Two from nothing you can't, but borrow twelve. Two from twelve, ten, and carry one. Please remember ten, sir, when I ask you. One from nothing you can't, borrow twenty. One from twenty, nineteen, and carry one. One from fifteen, fourteen. Fourteen pounds nineteen and — what did I tell you to remember?"

"Ten," said the General.

"Fourteen pounds nineteen shillings and ten-pence, then, is what I want," said Jackanapes.

"Bless my soul, what for?"

"To buy Lollo with. Lollo means red, sir. The Gypsy's red-haired pony, sir. Oh, he is beautiful! You should see his coat in the sun-
5 shine! You should see his mane! You should see his tail! Such little feet, sir, and they go like lightning! Such a dear face, too, and eyes like a mouse! But he's a racer, and the Gypsy wants fifteen pounds for him."

10   "If he's a racer, you couldn't ride him. Could you?"

"No—o, sir, but I can stick to him. I did the other day."

"You did, did you? Well, I'm fond of riding
15 myself, and if the beast is as good as you say, he might suit me."

"You're too tall for Lollo, I think," said Jackanapes, measuring his grandfather with his eye.

20   "I can double up my legs, I suppose. We'll have a look at him to-morrow."

"Don't you weigh a good deal?" asked Jackanapes.

"Chiefly waistcoats," said the General, slapping the breast of his military frock coat. "We'll have the little racer on the Green the first thing in the morning. Glad you mentioned it, grandson. Glad you mentioned it."

5

appropriateness (ap prō′prĭ ăt nes) : fitness

baptismal name (bap tiz′ml) : one's real name, given at baptism or christening ; also called Christian name

Chippendale (Chip′pn dāl) : a famous maker of furniture who lived over a hundred years ago

common : a piece of open land owned by the people of a town

conscientiously (kon′shĭ en′shus lў) : faithfully

desperate (des′pe rāt) : hopeless

dogs' ears : the rubbed and turned-over corners of the pages of a book

elastic (ēlas′tik) : springy

feasible (fēz′ĭ bl) : possible

gibbet (jĭb′bet) : a gallows ; a frame on which criminals were hanged

lattice (lat′tis) : crossed strips of thin wood over a window

military (mil′Ĭ tă rў) : soldiers

nimble : very active

scruples (skrū′plz) : objections to doing wrong

skittles (skit′tlz) : the old English game of ninepins

spurned : scorned

unceremoniously (un ser′ē mō′nĭ us-lў) : without formality, off-hand

vivid (vĭv′id) : very bright ; brilliant

wry (rī) : crooked, twisted

II

The General was as good as his word. Next morning the Gypsy and Lollo, Miss Jessamine, Jackanapes, and his grandfather and his dog Spitfire, were all gathered at one end of the Green in

a group, which so aroused the innocent curiosity
of Mrs. Johnson, as she saw it from one of her
upper windows, that she and the children took
their early promenade rather earlier than usual.
5 The General talked to the Gypsy, and Jackanapes
fondled Lollo's mane, and did not know whether
he should be more glad or miserable if his grandfather bought him.

"Jackanapes!"

10   "Yes, sir!"

"I've bought Lollo, but I believe you were right.
He hardly stands high enough for me.   If you can
ride him to the other end of the Green, I'll give
him to you."

15   How Jackanapes tumbled on to Lollo's back he
never knew.   He had just gathered up the reins
when the Gypsy-father took him by the arm.

"If you want to make Lollo go fast, my little
gentleman —"

20   "I can make him go!" said Jackanapes, and
drawing from his pocket the trumpet he had
bought in the fair, he blew a blast both loud and
shrill.

Away went Lollo, and away went Jackanapes' hat. His golden hair flew out, an aureole from which his cheeks shone red and distended with trumpeting. Away went Spitfire, mad with the rapture of the race, and the wind in his silky ears. 5 Away went the geese, the cocks, the hens, and the whole family of Johnson. Lucy clung to her mamma, Jane saved Emily by the gathers of her gown, and Tony saved himself by a somersault.

The Grey Goose was just returning when Jack- 10 anapes and Lollo rode back, Spitfire panting behind.

"Good, my little gentleman, good!" said the Gypsy. "You were born to the saddle. You've the flat thigh, the strong knee, the wiry back, and the light caressing hand; all you want is to learn 15 the whisper. Come here."

"What was that dirty fellow talking about, grandson?" asked the General.

"I can't tell you, sir. It's a secret."

They were sitting in the window again, in 20 the two Chippendale armchairs, the General devouring every line of his grandson's face, with strange spasms crossing his own.

"You must love your aunt very much, Jackanapes?"

"I do, sir," said Jackanapes warmly.

"And whom do you love next best to your aunt?"

5 The ties of blood were pressing very strongly
on the General himself, and perhaps he thought
of Lollo. But love is not bought in a day,
even with fourteen pounds nineteen shillings and
tenpence. Jackanapes answered quite readily,
10 "The Postman."

"Why the Postman?"

"He knew my father," said Jackanapes, "and
he tells me about him, and about his black mare.
My father was a soldier, a brave soldier. He
15 died at Waterloo. When I grow up, I want to
be a soldier too."

"So you shall, my boy, so you shall."

"Thank you, grandfather. Aunty doesn't
want me to be a soldier for fear of being killed."

20 "Bless my life! Would she have you stay in
a feather bed? Why, you might be killed by a
thunderbolt, if you were a butter merchant!"

"So I might. I shall tell her so. What a

funny fellow you are, sir! I say, do you think
my father knew the Gypsy's secret? The Postman says he used to whisper to his black mare."

"Your father was taught to ride as a child,
by one of those horsemen of the East who swoop 5
and dart and wheel about like swallows in autumn.
Grandson! Love me a little too. I can tell you
more about your father than the Postman can."

"I do love you," said Jackanapes. "Before
you came I was frightened. I'd no notion you 10
were so nice."

"Love me always, boy, whatever I do or
leave undone. And — God help me — whatever
you do or leave undone, I'll love you! There
shall never be a cloud between us for a day; 15
no, sir, not for an hour. We're imperfect enough,
all of us, we needn't be so bitter; and life is
uncertain enough at its safest; we needn't waste
its opportunities. Look at me! Here sit I, after
a dozen battles and some of the worst climates 20
in the world, and by yonder lych-gate lies your
mother, who didn't move five miles, I suppose,
from your aunt's apron strings, — dead in her

teens; my golden-haired daughter, whom I never saw."

Jackanapes was terribly troubled.

"Don't cry, grandfather," he pleaded, his own
5 blue eyes round with tears. "I will love you very much, and I will try to be very good. But I should like to be a soldier."

"You shall, my boy, you shall. You've more claims for a commission than you know of.
10 Cavalry, I suppose; eh, you young Jackanapes? Well, well; if you live to be an honor to your country, this old heart shall grow young again with pride for you; and if you die in the service of your country — well, it can but break for you!"

15   And beating the region which he said was all waistcoats, as if they stifled him, the old man got up and strode out on to the Green.

JULIANA H. EWING: *Jackanapes.*

aureole (ô're̅ ōl): a circle of light around the head; a halo

autumn (ô'tum): fall of the year

cavalry (kav'l ry̆): soldiers on horses

commission (kŏm mish'un): appointment as an officer in the army

devouring (dē vour'ing) eating up, taking in greedily

distended (dis tend'ed): stretched

fondled (fŏn'dld): touched tenderly

innocent (in'nō snt): harmless

lych-gate (lĭch'gāt): the gate or door to a graveyard

opportunities (op'per tū'nĭ tiz): chances

promenade (próm ē nād, *or* näd) : a
   walk

rapture (rap'chūr) : wild joy

spasms (spăzmz) : jerky motions of
   muscles that cannot be controlled

stifled (stī'fld) : smothered

Helps to Study

Mrs. Ewing's *Jackanapes* is a story of a brave and unselfish English boy. His mother had died when he was
a baby and his father had been killed in the battle of
Waterloo. You will want to read the rest of the book.
Though the ending is sad, it is a fine story of how Jackanapes gave his life for a friend while both of them were
fighting for their country.

I. 1. What are Gypsies? Where have you read of
them before? 2. Describe the pony Lollo. 3. How did
Jackanapes do on his first ride? 4. What was he to
remember when his grandfather came? 5. How did he
get on with his grandfather? 6. About what did they
talk? 7. Where do you see that Jackanapes is likely
to get the pony?

II. 1. Describe Jackanapes' ride on the pony.
2. "The whisper" is the special word the pony has been
taught that makes him run his fastest. 3. What shows
that the old General is proud of his grandson? 4. Why
does he say, "Cavalry, I suppose"? 5. What is meant
by the saying, "The ties of blood were pressing very
strongly on the General"? 6. How does the old man
show his deep feeling? 7. What do you think of Jackanapes?

THE CRUISE OF THE *DOLPHIN*

This story is based on facts, as are most of the things in Aldrich's famous book *The Story of a Bad Boy*. So well known is the book that many people go to Portsmouth, N.H., where the scenes of the book are laid, for the sake of seeing these scenes and the house where Aldrich spent his boyhood. You should read the whole book. Though this story is sad, most of the book is very amusing.

I

One afternoon the four owners of the *Dolphin* exchanged significant glances when Mr. Grimshaw announced from the desk that there would be no school the following day, he having just received
5 intelligence of the death of his uncle in Boston. I was sincerely attached to Mr. Grimshaw, but I am afraid that the death of his uncle did not affect me as it ought to have done.

We were up before sunrise the following morn-
10 ing in order to take advantage of the flood tide, which waits for no man. Our preparations for the cruise were made the previous evening. In the basket of eatables and drinkables, we had stored in the stern of the *Dolphin* a generous bag of
15 hard-tack (for the chowder), a piece of pork to

fry the cunners in, three gigantic apple pies, half
a dozen lemons, and a keg of spring water, — the
last named article we slung over the side, to keep
cool, as soon as we got under way. The crockery
and the bricks for our camp stove we placed in the
bows with the groceries, which included sugar,
pepper, salt, and a bottle of pickles. Phil Adams
contributed to the outfit a small tent of unbleached
cotton cloth, under which we intended to take our
nooning.

We unshipped the mast, threw in an extra oar,
and were ready to embark. I do not believe that
Christopher Columbus, when he started on his
rather successful voyage of discovery, felt half the
responsibility and importance that weighed upon
me as I sat on the middle seat of the *Dolphin*, with
my oar resting in the rowlock. I wonder if
Christopher Columbus quietly slipped out of the
house without letting his estimable family know
what he was up to ?

Charley Marden, whose father had promised to
cane him if he ever stepped foot on sail or row
boat, came down to the wharf in a sour-grape

humor, to see us off.   Nothing would tempt him
to go out on the river in such a crazy clamshell

of a boat.   He pretended that he did not expect to
behold us alive again, and tried to throw a wet
5 blanket over the expedition.

"Guess you'll have a squally time of it," said
Charley, casting off the painter.   "I'll drop in at
old Newbury's" (Newbury was the parish under-
taker) "and leave word as I go along!"

10   "Bosh!" muttered Phil Adams, sticking the
boat hook into the stringpiece of the wharf, and
sending the *Dolphin* half a dozen yards towards
the current.

How calm and lovely the river was!   Not a

ripple stirred on the glassy surface, broken only by the sharp cutwater of our tiny craft. The sun, as round and red as an August moon, was by this time peering above the water line.

The town had drifted behind us, and we were entering among the group of islands. Sometimes we could almost touch with our boat hook the shelving banks on either side. As we neared the mouth of the harbor, a little breeze now and then wrinkled the blue water, shook the spangles from the foliage, and gently lifted the spiral mist-wreaths that still clung along shore. The measured dip of our oars and the drowsy twitterings of the birds seemed to mingle with, rather than break, the enchanted silence that reigned about us.

The scent of the new clover comes back to me now, as I recall that delicious morning when we floated away in a fairy boat down a river like a dream!

The sun was well up when the nose of the *Dolphin* nestled against the snow-white bosom of Sandpeep Island. This island, as I have said before, was the last of the cluster, one side of it

being washed by the sea.   We landed on the river
side, the sloping sands and quiet water affording
us a good place to moor a boat.

It took us an hour or two to transport our stores
5 to the spot selected for the encampment.   Having
pitched our tent, using the five oars to support the
canvas, we got out our lines, and went down the

rocks seaward to fish.   It was early for cunners,
but we were lucky enough to catch as nice a mess
10 as ever you saw.   A cod for the chowder was not

so easily secured. At last Binny Wallace hauled in a plump little fellow crusted all over with flaky silver.

To skin the fish, build our fireplace, and cook the chowder kept us busy the next two hours. The fresh air and the exercise had given us the appetites of wolves, and we were about famished by the time the savory mixture was ready for our clamshell saucers.

I shall not insult the rising generation on the seaboard by telling them how delectable is a chowder compounded and eaten in this Robinson Crusoe fashion. As for the boys who live inland, and know naught of such marine feasts, my heart is full of pity for them. What wasted lives! Not to know the delights of a clambake, not to love chowder, to be ignorant of lobscouse!

How happy we were, we four, sitting cross-legged in the crisp salt grass, with the invigorating sea-breeze blowing gratefully through our hair! What a joyous thing was life, and how far off seemed death, — death, that lurks in all pleasant places, and was so near! ·

bows (bouz) : the front end of a boat

compounded (kom pound'ed) : mixed

craft (kraft) : any kind of small boat

cunner (kun'ner) : a small fish found in abundance in the sea off the New England coast

cutwater : track of a moving boat

delectable (dē lect'a bl) : enjoyable

embark (em bärk') : go on board

enchanted (en chant'ed) : magic

estimable (es'ti mā bl) : good, worthy of repect

expedition (eks'pe dish'un) : trip

gigantic (ji gan'tik) : very large

gratefully (grāt'ful lỹ) : pleasantly

hard-tack (härd'tăk) : a kind of hard biscuit

invigorating (in vig'er ā'ting) : strength-giving

lobscouse : a stew of meat and vegetables

marine (mā rēn') : belonging to the sea

moor (mo͞or) : to fasten

previous (prē'vĭ us) : before

rising generation (rīz'ing gen er ā'shun) : young people

rowlock (rō'lŏk) : the place on the side of a boat where the oar rests

savory (sā'ver ỹ) : sweet-smelling

seaboard (sē'bōrd) : sea-coast

significant (sig'nif'i knt) : full of meaning

sour-grape humor : do you remember the fable of the fox and the grapes?

stern : the rear end of a boat

transport (trans port') : to carry

unshipped (un shipt') : took down

II

The wind had freshened by this time, and we found it comfortable to put on the jackets which had been thrown aside in the heat of the day. We strolled along the beach and gathered large
5 quantities of the fairy-woven Iceland moss, which, at certain seasons, is washed to these shores; then we played at ducks and drakes, and then, the sun being sufficiently low, we went in bathing.

Before our bath was ended a slight change had
come over the sky and sea; fleecy-white clouds
scudded here and there, and a muffled moan from
the breakers caught our ears from time to time.
While we were dressing, a few hurried drops of 5
rain came lisping down, and we adjourned to the
tent to await the passing of the squall.

"We're all right, anyhow," said Phil Adams.
"It won't be much of a blow, and we'll be as snug
as a bug in a rug, here in the tent, particularly if 10
we have that lemonade which some of you fellows
were going to make."

By an oversight, the lemons had been left in the
boat.   Binny Wallace volunteered to go for them.

"Put an extra stone on the painter, Binny," 15
said Adams, calling after him; "it would be
awkward to have the *Dolphin* give us the slip and
return to port minus her passengers."

Sandpeep Island is diamond-shaped, — one
point running out into sea, and the other looking 20
towards the town.   Our tent and the *Dolphin* were
on the river side; but the *Dolphin* lay out of sight
by the beach at the farther extremity of the island.

WE SAW BINNY DRIFTING OUT TO SEA.

294

Binny Wallace had been absent five or six minutes, when we heard him calling our several names in tones that indicated distress or surprise, we could not tell which. Our first thought was, "The boat has broken adrift!"

We sprang to our feet and hastened down to the beach. On turning the bluff which hid the mooring place from our view, we found the conjecture correct. Not only was the *Dolphin* afloat, but poor little Binny Wallace was standing in the bows with his arms stretched helplessly towards us, — drifting out to sea!

"Head the boat in shore!" shouted Phil Adams.

Wallace ran to the tiller, but the slight cockleshell merely swung round and drifted broadside on. O, if we had but a single scull in the *Dolphin!*

"Can you swim it?" cried Adams, desperately, using his hand as a speaking-trumpet, for the distance between the boat and the island widened momently.

Binny Wallace looked down at the sea, which was covered with white caps, and made a despairing gesture. He knew, and we knew, that the stoutest swimmer could .not live forty seconds in those angry waters.

A wild, insane light came into Phil Adams's eyes, as he stood knee-deep in the boiling surf, 5 and for an instant I think he meditated plunging into the ocean after the receding boat.

The sky darkened, and an ugly look stole rapidly over the broken surface of the sea.

Binny. Wallace half rose from his seat in the 10 stern, and waved his hand to us in token of farewell. In spite of the distance, increasing every instant, we could see his face plainly. The anxious expression it wore at first had passed. It was pale and meek now, and I love to think 15 there was a kind of halo about it, like that which painters place around the forehead of a saint. So he drifted away.

The sky grew darker and darker. It was only by straining our eyes through the unnatural twi- 20 light that we could keep the *Dolphin* in sight. The figure of Binny Wallace was no longer visible, for the boat itself had dwindled to a mere white dot on the black water. Now we lost it, and our hearts stopped throbbing; and now the speck appeared again, for an instant, on the crest of a high wave.

Finally, it went out like a spark, and we saw it no more. Then we gazed at each other, and 5 dared not speak.

Absorbed in following the course of the boat, we had scarcely noticed the huddled inky clouds that sagged down all around us. From these threatening masses, seamed at intervals with pale 10 lightning, there now burst a heavy peal of thunder that shook the ground under our feet. A sudden squall struck the sea, ploughing deep white furrows into it, and at the same instant a single piercing shriek rose above the tempest, — the 15 frightened cry of a gull swooping over the island. How it startled us!

conjecture (con jek'chūr): guess

ducks and drakes: an old game, played with stones

extremity: (eks trem'i tў): end

halo (hā'lō): a band or circle of light around the head

meditated (med'i tāt'ed): thought of

minus (min'us): without

painter (pānt'er): the rope by which a boat is tied to the shore

receding (rē sēd'ing): going away

scull (skul): an oar

surf: waves breaking on the shore

tiller: the handle at the rear, by which a boat is steered

volunteered (vol'un tēr'd): offered

white caps: waves tipped with white, made when the wind blows hard

III

It was impossible any longer to keep our footing on the beach. The wind and the breakers would have swept us into the ocean if we had not clung to each other with the desperation of drowning men.

Taking advantage of a momentary lull, we crawled up the sands on our hands and knees, and, pausing in the lee of the granite ledge to gain breath, returned to the camp, where we found that the gale had snapped all the fastenings of the tent but one. Held by this, the puffed-out canvas swayed in the wind like a balloon. It was a task of some difficulty to secure it, which we did by beating down the canvas with the oars.

After several trials, we succeeded in setting up the tent on the leeward side of the ledge. Blinded by the vivid flashes of lightning, and drenched by the rain, which fell in torrents, we crept, half dead with fear and anguish, under our flimsy shelter. Neither the anguish nor the fear was on our own account, for we were comparatively safe, but for poor little Binny Wallace, driven out to

sea in the merciless gale. We shuddered to think
of him in that frail shell, drifting on and on to his
grave, the sky rent with lightning over his head,
and the green abysses yawning beneath him. We
fell to crying, the three of us, and cried I know
not how long.

Meanwhile the storm raged with augmented
fury. We were obliged to hold on to the ropes
of the tent to prevent its blowing away. The
spray from the river leaped several yards up the
rocks and clutched at us malignantly. The very
island trembled with the concussions of the sea
beating upon it, and at times I fancied that it had
broken loose from its foundation, and was floating
off with us. The breakers, streaked with angry
phosphorus, were fearful to look at.

The wind rose higher and higher, cutting long
slits in the tent, through which the rain poured
incessantly. To complete the sum of our miseries,
the night was at hand. It came down suddenly,
at last, like a curtain, shutting in Sandpeep Island
from all the world.

It was a dirty night, as the sailors say. The

darkness was something that could be felt as well as seen, — it pressed down upon one with a cold, clammy touch. Gazing into the hollow blackness, all sorts of imaginable shapes seemed to start
5 forth from vacancy, — brilliant colors, stars, prisms, and dancing lights. What boy, lying awake at night, has not amused or terrified himself by peopling the spaces around his bed with these phenomena of his own eyes?

0 "I say," whispered Fred Langdon, at length, clutching my hand, "don't you see things — out there — in the dark?"

"Yes, yes, — Binny Wallace's face!"

I added to my own nervousness by making this
5 avowal, though for the last ten minutes I had seen little besides that star-pale face with its angelic hair and brows. First a slim yellow circle, like the nimbus round the moon, took shape and grew sharp against the darkness; then this
0 faded gradually, and there was the Face, wearing the same sad, sweet look it wore when he waved his hand to us across the awful water. This optical illusion kept repeating itself.

"And I too," said Adams. "I see it every now and then, outside there. What wouldn't I give if it really was poor little Wallace looking in at us! O boys, how shall we dare to go back to the town without him? I've wished a hundred times, since we've been sitting here, that I was in his place, alive or dead!"

We dreaded the approach of morning as much as we longed for it. The morning would tell us all. Was it possible for the *Dolphin* to outride such a storm? There was a lighthouse on Mackerel Reef, which lay directly in the course the boat had taken, when it disappeared. If the *Dolphin* had caught on this reef, perhaps Binny Wallace was safe. Perhaps his cries had been heard by the keeper of the light. The man owned a lifeboat, and had rescued several people. Who could tell?

Such were the questions we asked ourselves again and again, as we lay in each other's arms waiting for daybreak. What an endless night it was! I have known months that did not seem so long.

abysses (ă bĭs'ez) : deep places

anguish (an'gwish) ; deep sorrow

augmented (aug ment'ed) : increased, greater

avowal (a vou'al) : confession

concussions (con cŭsh'shunz) : shocks

desperation (des'per ā'shun) : last hope

flimsy (flĭm'zў) : weak

incessantly (in ses'sant lў) : without stopping

lee (lē) : the sheltered side

maglignantly (ma lig'nant lў) : with a spirit of hatred

momentary (mō'men ta rў) : for a

moment, very short

nimbus (nim'bus) : a pale, cloud-like light

optical illusion (op'ti kal il lū'zhun) : a thing that appears to the eyes, but is not so

phenomena (fē nom'ē na) : appearances, things seen

phosphorus (fos'fŏr us) : certain creatures of the sea give off a light that is called phosphoric

vacancy (vā'kan sў) : empty space

yawning (yaun'ing) : opening, as for a victim

IV

Our position was irksome rather than perilous; for the day was certain to bring us relief from the town, where our prolonged absence, together with the storm, had no doubt excited the liveliest 5 alarm for our safety. But the cold, the darkness, and the suspense were hard to bear.

Our soaked jackets had chilled us to the bone. To keep warm, we lay huddled together so closely that we could hear our hearts beat above the 10 tumult of sea and sky.

After a while we grew very hungry, not having

broken our fast since early in the day. The rain had turned the hard-tack into a sort of dough, but it was better than nothing.

We used to laugh at Fred Langdon for always carrying in his pocket a small vial of essence of peppermint or sassafras, a few drops of which, sprinkled on a lump of loaf sugar, he seemed to consider a great luxury. I don't know what would have become of us at this crisis, if it hadn't been for the omnipresent bottle of hot stuff. We poured the stinging liquid over our sugar, which had kept dry in a sardine box, and warmed ourselves with frequent doses.

After four or five hours the rain ceased, the wind died away to a moan, and the sea — no longer raging like a maniac — sobbed and sobbed with a piteous human voice all along the coast. And well it might, after that night's work. Twelve sail of the Gloucester fishing fleet had gone down with every soul on board, just outside of Whale's-back Light. Think of the wide grief that follows in the wake of one wreck; then think of the despairing women who wrung their hands and wept the next morning in the streets of Gloucester, Marblehead, and Newcastle!

Though our strength was nearly spent, we were too cold to sleep. Once I sunk into a troubled 5 doze, when I seemed to hear Charley Marden's parting words, only it was the sea that said them. After that I threw off the drowsiness whenever it threatened to overcome me.

Fred Langdon was the earliest to discover a 10 filmy, luminous streak in the sky, the first glimmering of sunrise.

"Look, it is nearly daybreak!"

While we were following the direction of his finger, a sound of distant oars fell on our ears.

15 We listened breathlessly, and as the dip of the blades became more audible, we discerned two foggy lights, like will-o'-the-wisps, floating on the river.

Running down to the water's edge, we hailed 20 the boats with all our might. The call was heard, for the oars rested a moment in the rowlocks, and then pulled in towards the island.

It was two boats from the town, in the foremost

of which we could now make out the figures of
Captain Nutter and Binny Wallace's father. We
shrunk back on seeing him.

But when he saw only three boys standing on
the sands, his eye wandered restlessly about in 5
quest of the fourth; then a deadly pallor over-
spread his features.

Our story was soon told. A solemn silence fell
upon the crowd of rough boatmen gathered round,
interrupted only by a stifled sob from one poor 10
old man, who stood apart from the rest.

The sea was running too high for any small
boat to venture out; so it was arranged that the
wherry should take us back to town, leaving the
yawl, with a picked crew, to hug the island until 15
daybreak, and then set forth in search of the
Dolphin.

.   .   .   .

The excitement over, I was in a forlorn state,
physically and mentally. Captain Nutter put me
to bed between hot blankets, and sent for the doc- 20
tor. I was wandering in my mind, and fancied
myself still on Sandpeep Island: now we were

U

building our brick stove to cook the chowder, and, in my delirium, I laughed aloud and shouted to my comrades; now the sky darkened and the squall struck the island; now I gave orders to
5 Wallace how to manage the boat, and now I cried because the rain was pouring in on me through the holes in the tent. Towards evening a high fever set in, and it was many days before my grandfather deemed it prudent to tell me that the
10 *Dolphin* had been found floating keel upwards, four miles southwest of Mackerel Reef.

. . . .

What a pang shot across my heart the afternoon it was whispered through the town that a body had been washed ashore at Grave Point, —
15 the place where we bathed. We bathed there no more! How well I remember the funeral, and what a piteous sight it was afterwards to see his familiar name on a small headstone in the Old South Burying Ground!

THOMAS BAILEY ALDRICH: *The Story of a Bad Boy.*
(ADAPTED.)

audible (aud'i bl) : that can be heard

discerned (diz zernd') : saw, made out

interrupted (in'ter rupt'ed) : broken into

irksome (erk'sum) : tiresome

luminous (lū'mi nus) : clear, shining

luxury (luk'shu ry) : something very fine and good

maniac (mā'nǐ ǎk) : a crazy person

omnipresent (om'nǐ prez'nt) : always on hand

pallor (păl'ler) : paleness

perilous (per'i lus) : dangerous

stifled (stī'fld) : smothered, kept back

suspense (sus pens') : anxious or worried waiting

twelve sail : twelve ships

tumult (tū'mult) : noise and confusion

wherry (hwer'ry) : a long, narrow, light boat

yawl (yaul) : a small boat

Helps to Study

I. 1. Why does the author say that he was not much affected by the death of Mr. Grimshaw's uncle? 2. On page 286, line 11, there is an old proverb referred to. What is it? 3. What preparations did the boys make for their outing? 4. On the same page there is a hint that our boy slipped off without permission: find it. 5. What is meant by "throwing a wet blanket over the expedition"? 6. What work had the boys to do at their camping-place? 7. Explain the phrase, "Robinson Crusoe fashion."

II. 1. Why did the boys wait until the sun was low to go in bathing? 2. How did Binny come to be lost? 3. What warning had he forgotten? 4. Why could he not be saved? 5. What was the last the others saw of him?

III. 1. Tell about the night and the storm that followed. 2. What other sorrows had this same night brought?

IV. 1. How did they feel about going back to the town? 2. How did Binny's father know his boy was lost?

THE SKATING RACE

Hans Brinker is another of the books that every boy and girl ought to know. The scene is laid in Holland, and tells many interesting things about the life and customs of the Dutch. Skating is one of their favorite sports, and prizes are given for the best boy and girl skaters. Hans and his sister Gretel are a pair that you will be glad to know better.

I

A flag is waved from the judges' stand. Madame Van Gleck rises in her pavilion. She leans forward with a white handkerchief in her hand. When she drops it, a bugler is to give the 5 signal for them to start. The handkerchief is fluttering to the ground. Hark! They are off! No. Back again. Their line was not true in passing the judges' stand. The signal is repeated. Off again. No mistake this time. Whew! how fast 10 they go! The multitude is quiet for an instant, absorbed in eager, breathless watching. Cheers spring up along the line of spectators. Huzza! five girls are ahead. Who comes flying back from the boundary mark? We cannot tell. Some-15 thing red, that is all. There is a blue spot flitting

near it, and a dash of yellow nearer still. Spectators at this end of the line strain their eyes and wish they had taken their post nearer the flagstaff. The wave of cheers is coming back again. Now we can see! Katrinka is ahead! 5

She passes the Van Holp pavilion. The next is Madame van Gleck's. That leaning figure gazing from it is a magnet. Hilda shoots past Katrinka, waving her hand to her mother as she passes. Two others are close now, whizzing on 10

like arrows.   What is that flash of red and gray?
Hurrah, it is Gretel!   She, too, waves her hand
but toward no gay pavilion.   The crowd is cheering, but she hears only her father's voice, "Well
5 done, little Gretel!"   Soon Katrinka, with a quick
merry laugh, shoots past Hilda.   The girl in yellow is gaining now.   She passes them all, all
except Gretel.   The judges lean forward without
seeming to lift their eyes from their watches.
10 Cheer after cheer fills the air; the very columns
seem rocking.   Gretel has passed them.   She has
won.

"Gretel Brinker — one mile!" — shouts the crier.
The judges nod.   They write something upon a
15 tablet which each holds in his hand.

While the girls are resting — some crowding
eagerly around our frightened little Gretel, some
standing aside in high disdain — the boys form in
a line.   Mynheer van Gleck drops the handker-
20 chief this time.   The buglers give a vigorous
blast! The boys have started.   Half way already!
Did ever you see the like!   Three hundred legs
flashing by in an instant.   But there are only

twenty boys. No matter, there were hundreds of legs I am sure! Where are they now? There is such a noise one gets bewildered. What are the people laughing at? Oh, at that fat boy in the rear. See him go! See him! He'll be down in 5 an instant; no, he won't. I wonder if he knows he is all alone; the other boys are nearly at the boundary line. Yes, he knows it. He stops! He wipes his hot face. He takes off his cap and looks about him. Better to give up 10 with a good grace. He has made a hundred friends by that hearty, astonished laugh. Good Jacob Poot! The fine fellow is already among the spectators gazing as eagerly as the rest. 15

A cloud of feathery ice flies from the heels of the skaters as they "bring to" and turn at the flagstaffs. Something black is coming now, one of the boys — it is all we know. He has touched the feelings of the crowd; it fairly roars. Now 20 they come nearer — we can see the red cap. There's Ben — there's Peter — there's Hans! Hans is ahead! Young Madame Van Gend almost crushes the flowers in her hand; she had been quite sure that Peter would be first. Carl Schummel is next, then Ben, and the youth with the red cap. The others are pressing close. A 5 tall figure darts from among them. He passes the red cap, he passes Ben, then Carl. Now it is an even race between him and Hans. Madame Van Gend catches her breath.

It is Peter! He is ahead! Hans shoots past 10 him. Hilda's eyes fill with tears, Peter must beat. Annie's eyes flash proudly. Gretel gazes with clasped hands — four strokes more will take her brother to the columns. He is there! Yes, but so was young Schummel just a second before. At 15 the last instant, Carl, gathering his powers, had whizzed between them and passed the goal.

"Carl Schummel! One mile!" shouts the crier.

bewildered (bē wil′derd): muddled, confused

disdain (dis dān′): pride and scorn

magnet (mag′net): something that has the power to draw things to itself

multitude (mul′ti tūd): crowd

pavilion (pa vil′yun): a platform covered by a roof, but open at the sides

spectators (spek tā′terz): lookers-on

II

Soon Madame Van Gleck rises again. The falling handkerchief starts the bugle; and the bugle, using its voice as a bowstring, shoots off twenty girls like so many arrows. It is a beautiful sight, but one has not long to look; before we can fairly distinguish them they are far in the distance. This time they are close upon one another; it is hard to say, as they come speeding back from the flagstaff, which will reach the columns first. There are new faces among the foremost — eager, glowing faces, unnoticed before. Katrinka is there and Hilda, but Gretel and Rychie are in the rear. Gretel is wavering, but when Rychie passes her, she starts forward afresh. Now they are nearly beside Katrinka. Hilda is still in advance; she is almost "home." She has not faltered since that bugle note sent her flying; like an arrow still she is speeding toward the goal. Cheer after cheer rises in the air. Peter is silent, but his eyes shine like stars. "Huzza! huzza!" The crier's voice is heard again.

" Hilda van Gleck, one mile ! "

A loud murmur of approval runs through the crowd catching the music in its course, till all seems one sound, with a glad rhythmic throbbing
5 in its depths. When the flag waves all is still. Once more the bugle blows a terrific blast. It sends off the boys like chaff before the wind — dark chaff I admit, and in big pieces. It is whisked around at the flagstaff, driven faster yet
10 by the cheers and shouts along the line. We begin to see what is coming. There are three boys in advance this time, and all abreast. Hans, Peter, and Lambert. Carl soon breaks the ranks, rushing through with a whiff! Fly Hans, fly
15 Peter. Don't let Carl beat again — Carl the bitter, Carl the insolent. Van Mounen is flagging, but you are strong as ever. Hans and Peter, Peter and Hans; which is foremost? We love them both. We scarcely care which is the fleeter.
20 Hilda, Annie, and Gretel seated upon the long crimson bench can remain quiet no longer. They spring to their feet — so different, and yet one in eagerness. Hilda instantly reseats herself; none

shall know how interested she is, none shall know how anxious, how filled with one hope. Shut your eyes then, Hilda — hide your face rippling with joy. Peter has beaten.

"Peter van Holp, one mile!" calls the crier. 5

The same buzz of excitement as before, while the judges take notes, the same throbbing of music through the din — but something is different. A little crowd presses close about some object. near the columns. Carl has fallen. He is 10

not hurt, though somewhat stunned. If he were
less sullen he would find more sympathy in these
warm young hearts. As it is they forget him as
soon as he is fairly on his feet again. The girls
5 are to skate their third mile. How resolute the
little maidens look as they stand in a line! Some
are solemn with a sense of responsibility, some
wear a smile half bashful, half provoked, but one
air of determination pervades them all. This third
10 mile may decide the race. Still if neither Gretel
nor Hilda win, there is yet a chance among the
rest for the Silver Skates. Each girl feels sure
that this time she will accomplish the distance in
one half the time. How they stamp to try their
15 runners, how nervously they examine each strap,
— how erect they stand at last, every eye upon
Madame Van Gleck!

The bugle thrills through them again. With
quivering eagerness they spring forward, bending,
20 but in perfect balance. Each flashing stroke
seems longer than the last. Now they are skimming off in the distance. Again the eager straining of eyes — again the shouts and cheering, again

the thrill of excitement as, after a few moments, four or five, in advance of the rest, come speeding, back, nearer, nearer to the white columns. Who is first? Not Rychie, Katrinka, Annie, nor Hilda, nor the girl in yellow — but Gretel — Gretel, the fleetest sprite of a girl that ever skated. She was but playing in the earlier race, now she is in earnest, or rather something within her has determined to win. That lithe little form makes no effort; but it cannot stop — not until the goal is passed! In vain the crier lifts his voice — he cannot be heard. He has no news to tell — it is already ringing through the crowd. Gretel has won the Silver Skates!

Like a bird she has flown over the ice, like a bird she looks about her in a timid, startled way. She longs to dart to the sheltered nook where her father and mother stand. But Hans is beside her — the girls are crowding round. Hilda's kind, joyous voice breathes in her ear. From that hour, none will despise her. Goose-girl or not, Gretel stands acknowledged Queen of the Skaters!

MARY MAPES DODGE: *Hans Brinker,
or the Silver Skates* (ADAPTED).

accomplish (ak kom'plish) : to make
faltered (fal'ter'd) : weakened
fleeter (flēt'er) : swifter
insolent (in'sŏl ent) : proud and rude

lithe (lith) : graceful and strong
rhythmic (rith'mik) : with regular
  and even beats
sprite (sprīt) : spirit, fairy

Helps to Study

1. What part of this story of the race do you like best?
2. Would you not like it better if you knew more about
the boys and girls who are in the race? You can do so by
reading the book, *Hans Brinker*. 3. Tell about some
game or contest for a prize that you have seen or taken
part in.

Review Questions

1. What was the real name of Jackanapes? What was
he told to do or not to do when his grandfather came?
How did they get on together? What did they talk
about? What did the General do for him?

2. Where did the boys live who went on the *Dolphin?*
What sad accident happened? Tell about it.

3. Who took part in the skating race? Who won the
silver skates?

WOODMAN, SPARE THAT TREE

Woodman, spare that tree!
  Touch not a single bough!
In youth it sheltered me,
  And I'll protect it now.
'Twas my forefather's hand   5
  That placed it near his cot:
There, woodman, let it stand;
  Thy ax shall harm it not.

That old familiar tree,
  Whose glory and renown   10
Are spread o'er land and sea, —
  And wouldst thou hew it down?
Woodman, forbear thy stroke;
  Cut not its earth-bound ties:
O, spare that aged oak   15
  Now towering to the skies!

When but an idle boy
  I sought its grateful shade;
In all their gushing joy
  Here too my sisters played.   20

My mother kissed me here,
    My father pressed my hand:
Forgive this foolish tear,
    But let that old oak stand!

5   My heart-strings round thee cling,
    Close as thy bark, old friend!
Here shall the wild bird sing,
    And still thy branches bend.
Old tree, the storm still brave!
10   And, woodman, leave the spot:
While I've a hand to save,
    Thy ax shall harm it not.

GEORGE P. MORRIS.

cot: here used for cottage   renown (rē noun'): fame

HELPS TO STUDY

1. Trees are among the most beautiful, as well as useful, gifts of nature. How long does it take to make a good tree? 2. What kind of tree is this one? 3. Why does the poet want the tree saved? 4. What memories about it does he have? Who planted it? Who played under it?

LITTLE DAFFYDOWNDILLY

I

Daffydowndilly was so called because he was like a flower, and loved to do only what was agreeable, and took no delight in labor of any kind.

But while Daffydowndilly was yet a little boy, [5] his mother sent him away from home and put him under the care of a very strict schoolmaster, who went by the name of Mr. Toil. Those who knew him best said that this Mr. Toil was a very good man and had done more good, both [10] to children and grown people, than anybody else in the world.

Yet Mr. Toil had a severe and ugly face, especially for such little boys or big men as were idle. His voice, too, was harsh. All his [15] ways seemed very disagreeable to our friend Daffydowndilly.

The whole day long the old schoolmaster sat at his desk overlooking the children, or stalked about the schoolroom with a birch rod in his [20] hand.   Unless a lad chose to attend to his book, he had no chance of enjoying a quiet moment.

"This will never do for me," said Daffydowndilly to himself when he had been at school 5 about a week. "I'll run away and try to find my dear mother. At any rate, I shall never find anybody half so disagreeable as this old Mr. Toil."

So, the very next morning, off started poor 10 Daffydowndilly. He had gone only a short distance, when he overtook a man who was trudging along the road.

"Good morning, my fine lad," said the stranger, and his voice seemed hard and severe, but yet 15 had a sort of kindness in it; "whence do you come so early and whither are you going?"

Little Daffydowndilly had never been known to tell a lie in all his life. Nor did he tell one now. He hesitated a moment or two, but at 20 last confessed that he had run away from school on account of his great dislike for Mr. Toil.

"Oh, very well, my little friend!" answered the stranger. "Then we will go together. I,

too, have had a good deal to do with Mr. Toil,
and shall be glad to find some place where he
was never heard of."

Our friend Daffydowndilly would have been
better pleased with some one of his own age, 5
with whom he might have gathered flowers along
the roadside, or have chased butterflies, or have
done other things to make the journey pleasant.
But he agreed to go with the stranger, and
they walked on together. ·   10

They had not gone far, when the road passed
by a field where some haymakers were at work.
Daffydowndilly was delighted with the sweet
smell of the hay. He thought how much pleas-
anter it must be to make hay in the sunshine, 15
under the blue sky, than to be shut up in a
schoolroom with old Mr. Toil; but while he was
stopping to peep over the stone wall, he started
back and caught hold of his companion's hand.

"Quick, quick!" cried he. "Let us run away, 20
or he will catch us!"

"Who will catch us?" asked the stranger.

"Mr. Toil, the old schoolmaster!" answered

Daffydowndilly.   "Don't you see him among the haymakers?"

And Daffydowndilly pointed to an old man, who seemed to be the employer of the men at
5 work there.   He was busily at work in his shirt-sleeves.   The drops of sweat stood upon his brow; but he gave himself not a moment's rest, and kept crying out to the haymakers to make hay while the sun shone.   Now, strange
10 to say, this old farmer looked just like old Mr. Toil.

"Don't be afraid," said the stranger.   "This is not Mr. Toil the schoolmaster, but a brother of his.   People say he is the more disagreeable
15 man of the two.   However, he won't trouble you unless you become a laborer on the farm."

Yet little Daffydowndilly was very glad when they were out of sight of the old farmer, who looked so much like Mr. Toil.

II

20 Then they went on a little farther, and soon heard the sound of a drum and fife.   Daffydown-

MR. TOIL AMONG THE SOLDIERS.

dilly begged his companion to hurry forward, that they might not miss seeing the soldiers.

So they made what haste they could, and soon met a company of soldiers, gayly dressed, with 5 muskets on their shoulders. In front marched two drummers and two fifers, making such lively music that little Daffydowndilly would gladly have followed them to the end of the world. And if he were only a soldier, then, he said to himself, 10 old Mr. Toil would never dare look him in the face.

"Forward, march!" shouted a gruff voice.

Little Daffydowndilly started in great dismay. This voice which had spoken to the soldiers sounded just like that which he had heard every 15 day in Mr. Toil's schoolroom, out of Mr. Toil's own mouth.

Turning his eyes to the captain of the company, what should he see but the very image of Mr. Toil himself, in a fine uniform, with a long sword, 20 instead of a birch rod, in his hand. In spite of all this, he looked quite as ugly and disagreeable as when he was hearing lessons in the schoolroom.

"This is certainly old Mr. Toil," said Daffydowndilly in a trembling voice. "Let us run away."

"You are mistaken again, my little friend," replied the stranger. "This is not Mr. Toil the schoolmaster, but a brother of his who has served in the army all his life. People say he's a very severe fellow, but you and I need not be afraid of him."

"Well, well," said little Daffydowndilly, "but, if you please, sir, I don't want to see the soldiers any more."

So the child and the stranger went on.

By and by they came to a house by the roadside, where a number of people were making merry. Young men and rosy-cheeked girls were dancing to the sound of a fiddle. It was the pleasantest sight that Daffydowndilly had yet met with.

"Oh, let us stop here," cried he to his companion, "for Mr. Toil will never dare show his face where there is a fiddler, and where people are dancing and making merry. We shall be quite safe here!"

But these last words died away upon Daffydowndilly's tongue. Happening to cast his eyes
on the fiddler, whom should he see again but the
likeness of Mr. Toil, holding a fiddle bow instead
5 of a birch rod. Daffydowndilly even fancied that
he nodded and winked at him, and made signs for
him to join in the dance.

"Oh, dear me!" whispered he, turning pale,
"it seems as if there was nobody but Mr. Toil in
10 the world. Who could have thought of his playing on a fiddle?"

"This is not your old schoolmaster," said the
stranger, "but another brother of his, who is a fiddler. He is ashamed of his family, and generally
15 calls himself Mr. Pleasure. But his real name is
Toil, and those who have known him best think
him still more disagreeable than his brother."

"Let us go a little farther," said Daffydowndilly. "I don't like the looks of this fiddler at all."
20 Well, thus the stranger and little Daffydowndilly went wandering along the highway, and in
shady lanes and through pleasant villages.

Wherever they went, there was the image of

old Mr. Toil. He stood like a scarecrow in the cornfields. If they entered a house, he sat in the parlor. If they peeped into the kitchen, he was there. He made himself at home in every cottage, and stole, in one shape or another, into the 5 finest houses. Everywhere there was sure to be one of the old schoolmaster's many hard-working brothers.

III

Little Daffydowndilly was almost tired to death, when he saw some people lying in a shady place 10 by the side of the road. The poor child begged his companion that they might sit down there and take some rest.

"Old Mr. Toil will never come here," said he, "for he hates to see people taking their ease." 15

But, even while he spoke, Daffydowndilly's eyes fell upon a person who seemed the laziest of all those lazy people who had lain down to sleep in the shade. Who should it be again but the very image of Mr. Toil! 20

"There is a large family of these Toils," said

the stranger. "This is another of the old school-master's brothers, who has very idle habits and goes by the name of Mr. Do Nothing. He pretends to lead an easy life, but is really the most 5 miserable fellow in the family."

"Oh, take me back! take me back!" cried poor little Daffydowndilly, bursting into tears. "If there is nothing but Toil all over the world, I may just as well go back to the schoolhouse!"

10 "There it is — there is the schoolhouse," said the stranger; for though he and little Daffydowndilly had taken a great many steps, they had traveled in a circle instead of a straight line. "Come, we will go back to school together."

15 There was something in his companion's voice that little Daffydowndilly now remembered; and it is strange that he had not remembered it sooner. Looking up into his face, there again was the likeness of old Mr. Toil. The poor child 20 had been in company with Toil all day, even while he was doing his best to run away from him.

Some people, who have heard little Daffydowndilly's story, believe that old Mr. Toil was a magician and that he could change himself into any shape.

Be this as it may, little Daffydowndilly had learned a good lesson, and from that time forward he worked at his task, because he knew that work 5 is no more toilsome than sport or idleness.

And when he knew Mr. Toil better, he began to think that his ways were not so very disagreeable, and that his smile of approval made his face almost as pleasant as even that of Daffydown- 10 dilly's mother.

NATHANIEL HAWTHORNE.

approval (ap prōōv'l) : liking, thinking well of
Daffydowndilly (daf'fy down dil'ly) : daffodil. See page 103.

dismay (dis mā') : fright
hesitated (hez'i tāted) : paused, delayed

HELPS TO STUDY

1. Why did Daffydowndilly run away from school? 2. What different groups of people did he see on his walk? 3. What person that he did not wish to see was in each group? 4. Who did his companion prove to be? 5. What lesson did the boy learn? 6. What lesson has the story for you?

CASABIANCA

The boy stood on the burning deck,
　Whence all but him had fled;
The flame that lit the battle's wreck
　Shone round him o'er the dead.

5　Yet beautiful and bright he stood,
　　As born to rule the storm;

A creature of heroic blood,
    A proud though childlike form.

The flames rolled on — he would not go
    Without his father's word;
That father, faint in death below,   5
    His voice no longer heard.

He called aloud, "Say, father, say
    If yet my task is done?"
He knew not that the chieftain lay
    Unconscious of his son.   10

"Speak, father!" once again he cried,
    "If I may yet be gone!"
And but the booming shots replied,
    And fast the flames rolled on.

Upon his brow he felt their breath,   15
    And in his waving hair;
And looked from that lone post of death,
    In still, yet brave despair.

And shouted but once more aloud
    "My father! must I stay?"   20

While o'er him fast, through sail and shroud,
    The wreathing fires made way.

They wrapt the ship in splendor wild,
    They caught the flag on high,
5 And streamed above the gallant child
    Like banners in the sky.

Then came a burst of thunder sound —
    The boy — oh! where was he?
 — Ask of the winds that far around
10   With fragments strew the sea;

With mast, and helm, and pennon fair,
    That well had borne their part —
But the noblest thing that perished there
    Was that young, faithful heart.

FELICIA HEMANS.

HELPS TO STUDY

1. This is a famous poem, which every one is supposed to know.   2. What is the scene of it?   3. Where is the boy?   4. Why does he stay?   5. Where is his father?

HOME, SWEET HOME

1. 'Mid pleas-ures and pal a-ces . though we may roam,
2. An ex - ile from home, splendor daz - zles in vain;

Be it ev - er so hum - ble, there's no place like home; A
O give me my low - ly thatched cot - tage a - gain! The

charm from the sky seems to hal - low us there, Which, seek through the
birds sing-ing gai - ly, that came at my call, Give me them, and the

CHORUS

world, is ne'er met with else-where. Home! Home! sweet, sweet
peace of mind, dear - er than all.

Home! There's no place like Home, there's no place like Home.

How sweet 'tis to sit 'neath a fond father's smile,
And the cares of a mother to soothe and beguile!
Let others delight 'mid new pleasures to roam,
But give me, oh, give me, the pleasures of home!

Home! home! sweet, sweet home!
There's no place like home! there's no place like
home!

To thee I'll return, overburdened with care;
The heart's dearest solace will smile on me there;
No more from that cottage again will I roam;
Be it ever so humble, there's no place like home.

5 Home! home! sweet, sweet home!
There's no place like home! there's no place like
    home!

JOHN HOWARD PAYNE.

---

beguile (bē gīl'): to charm away

hallow (hal'lō): to make beautiful or sacred

'mid: a short form of amid, meaning among

'neath: beneath

thatched (thachd): roofed with straw

solace (sŏl'as): comfort

HELPS TO STUDY

The author of this well-known poem was an American, who died in 1800. His own life ended in wandering and poverty.

A MAD TEA-PARTY

There was a table set out under a tree in front
of the house, and the March Hare and the Hatter were having tea at it: a Dormouse was sitting
between them, fast asleep, and the other two were
using it as a cushion, resting their elbows on it, 5
and talking over its head. "Very uncomfortable
for the Dormouse," thought Alice; "only as it's
asleep I suppose it doesn't mind."

The table was a large one, but the three
were all crowded together at one corner of it. 10
"No room! No room!" they cried out when
they saw Alice coming. "There's *plenty* of
room!" said Alice, indignantly, and she sat
down in a large arm-chair at one end of the
table.   15

"Have some wine," the March Hare said, in an
encouraging tone.

Alice looked all round the table, but there was
nothing on it but tea. "I don't see any wine,"
she remarked.   20

"There isn't any," said the March Hare.

Y   337

He Poured Some Hot Tea on Its Nose.

"Then it wasn't very civil of you to offer it," said Alice, angrily.

"It wasn't very civil of you to sit down without being invited," said the March Hare.

"I didn't know it was *your* table," said Alice; "it's laid for a great many more than three."

"You should learn not to make personal remarks," Alice said with some severity; "it's very rude."

The Hatter opened his eyes very wide on hearing this; but all he *said* was, "Why is a raven like a writing-desk?"

"Come, we shall have some fun now!" thought Alice. "I'm glad they've begun asking riddles — I believe I can guess that," she added aloud.

"Do you mean that you think you can find out the answer to it?" said the March Hare.

"Exactly so," said Alice.

"Then you should say what you mean," the March Hare went on.

"I do," Alice hastily replied; "at least — at least I mean what I say — that's the same thing, you know."

"Not the same thing a bit!" said the Hatter. "Why, you might just as well say that 'I see what I eat' is the same thing as 'I eat what I see'!"

5 "You might just as well say," added the Dormouse, who seemed to be talking in his sleep, "that 'I breathe when I sleep' is the same thing as 'I sleep when I breathe'!"

"It *is* the same thing with you," said the Hat-
10 ter, and here the conversation dropped, and the party sat silent for a minute, while Alice thought over all she could remember about ravens and writing-desks, which wasn't much.

"Have you guessed the riddle yet?" the Hatter
15 said, turning to Alice again.

"No, I give it up," Alice replied. "What's the answer?"

"I haven't the slightest idea," said the Hatter.

"Nor I," said the March Hare.

20 Alice sighed wearily. "I think you might do something better with the time," she said, "than wasting it in asking riddles that have no answers."

"If you knew Time as well as I do," said the Hatter, "you wouldn't talk about wasting *it*. It's *him*."

"I don't know what you mean," said Alice.

"Of course you don't!" the Hatter said, toss-5 ing his head contemptuously. "I dare say you never spoke to Time!"

"Perhaps not," Alice cautiously replied; "but I know I have to beat time when I learn music."

"Ah! That accounts for it," said the Hatter. 10 "He won't stand beating. Now, if you only kept on good terms with him, he'd do almost anything you liked with the clock. For instance, suppose it were nine o'clock in the morning, just time to begin lessons: you'd only have to whis-15 per a hint to Time, and round goes the clock in a twinkling! Half-past one, time for dinner!"

("I only wish it was," the March Hare said to itself in a whisper.)

"That would be grand, certainly," said Alice, 20 thoughtfully: "but then — I shouldn't be hungry for it, you know."

"Not at first, perhaps," said the Hatter; "but

you could keep it to half-past one as long as you liked."

"Is that the way *you* manage?" Alice asked.

The Hatter shook his head mournfully. "Not I," he replied. "We quarreled last March — just before *he* went mad, you know —" (pointing with his teaspoon at the March Hare) "— it was at the great concert given by the Queen of Hearts, and I had to sing:

> "'Twinkle, twinkle, little bat!
> How I wonder what you're at!'

You know the song, perhaps?"

"I've heard something like it," said Alice.

"It goes on, you know," the Hatter continued, "in this way:

> "'Up above the world you fly,
> Like a tea-tray in the sky.
> Twinkle, twinkle —'"

Here the Dormouse shook itself, and began singing in his sleep, "*Twinkle, twinkle, twinkle, twinkle,* —" and went on so long that they had to pinch it to make it stop.

"Well, I'd hardly finished the first verse," said the Hatter, "when the Queen bawled out: 'He's murdering the time! Off with his head!'"

"How dreadfully savage!" exclaimed Alice.

"And ever since that," the Hatter went on in a mournful tone, "he won't do a thing I ask! It's always six o'clock now."

"Suppose we change the subject," the March Hare interrupted, yawning. "I'm getting tired of this. I vote the young lady tells us a story."

"I'm afraid I don't know one," said Alice, rather alarmed at the proposal.

"Then the Dormouse shall!" they both cried. "Wake up, Dormouse!" And they pinched it on both sides at once.

The Dormouse slowly opened its eyes. "I wasn't asleep," it said in a hoarse, feeble voice, "I heard every word you fellows were saying."

"Tell us a story!" said the March Hare.

"Yes, please do!" pleaded Alice.

"And be quick about it," added the Hatter, "or you'll be asleep again before it's done."

"Once upon a time there were three little

sisters," the Dormouse began in a great hurry; " and their names were Elsie, Lacie, and Tillie; and they lived at the bottom of a well —"

"What did they live on?" said Alice, who 5 always took a great interest in questions of eating and drinking.

"They lived on treacle," said the Dormouse, after thinking a minute or two.

"They couldn't have done that, you know," 10 Alice gently remarked: "they'd have been ill."

"So they were," said the Dormouse; " *very* ill."

Alice tried a little to fancy to herself what such an extraordinary way of living would be like, but it puzzled her too much, so she went on, " But 15 why did they live at the bottom of a well?"

" Take some more tea," the March Hare said to Alice, very earnestly.

" I've had nothing yet," Alice replied in an offended tone, " so I can't take more."

20 " You mean, you can't take *less*," said the Hatter; " it's very easy to take *more* than nothing."

" Nobody asked *your* opinion," said Alice.

"Who's making personal remarks now?" the Hatter asked triumphantly.

Alice did not quite know what to say to this: so she helped herself to some tea and bread-and-butter, and then turned to the Dormouse, and repeated her question. "Why did they live at the bottom of a well?"

The Dormouse again took a minute or two to think about it, and then said, "It was a treaclewell."

"There's no such thing!" Alice was beginning very angrily; but the Hatter and the March Hare went "Sh! sh!" and the Dormouse sulkily remarked, "If you can't be civil you'd better finish the story for yourself."

"No, please go on!" Alice said very humbly. "I won't interrupt you again. I dare say there may be *one*."

"One, indeed!" said the Dormouse, indignantly. However, he consented to go on. "And so these three little sisters — they were learning to draw, you know —"

"What did they draw?" said Alice, quite forgetting her promise.

"Treacle," said the Dormouse, without considering at all this time.

Alice did not wish to offend the Dormouse again, so she began very cautiously: "But I
5 don't understand. Where did they draw the treacle from?"

"You can draw water out of a water-well," said the Hatter; "so I should think you could draw treacle out of a treacle-well — eh, stupid?"

10 "But they were *in* the well," Alice said to the Dormouse, not choosing to notice this last remark.

"Of course they were," said the Dormouse; "well in."

15 This answer so confused poor Alice, that she let the Dormouse go on for some time without interrupting it.

"They were learning to draw," the Dormouse went on, yawning and rubbing its eyes, for it
20 was getting very sleepy; "and they drew all manner of things — everything that begins with an M —"

"Why with an M?" said Alice.

"Why not?" said the March Hare.

Alice was silent.

The Dormouse had closed its eyes by this time, and was going off into a doze; but, on being pinched by the Hatter, it woke up again with [5] a little shriek, and went on: "— that begins with an M, such as mouse-traps, and the moon, and memory, and muchness — you know you say things are 'much of a muchness' — did you ever see such a thing as a drawing of a much- [10] ness?"

"Really, now you ask me," said Alice, very much confused, "I don't think —"

"Then you shouldn't talk," said the Hatter.

This piece of rudeness was more than Alice could [15] bear; she got up in great disgust and walked off. The last time she saw them, they were trying to put the Dormouse into the teapot.

"At any rate I'll never go there again!" said Alice, as she picked her way through the wood. [20] "It's the stupidest tea-party I ever was at in all my life!"

LEWIS CARROLL: *Alice's Adventures in Wonderland.*

civil (siv'il) : polite

dormouse : a small animal that burrows underground

indignantly (in dig'nant lỷ) : angrily

o'clock : a short form of saying *of the clock*, used in telling the time of day

severity (se ver'ĭ tỷ) : sternness

treacle (trē'kl) : molasses

HELPS TO STUDY

In England, the afternoon tea, about five o'clock, is as important as breakfast or dinner. Everybody has it, and usually with bread-and-butter and jam.

1. Who are at the table? 2. There are three common expressions that suggest the characters for this scene: As mad as a March hare. As mad as a hatter. To sleep like a dormouse. The dormouse does indeed sleep a great deal. It hibernates; that is, sleeps through the winter, as the bear does.

3. How do the people at the table welcome Alice? 4. What puzzling, nonsensical things do they say? 5. What do they do to the dormouse? 6. Where does Alice go at the end of the scene?

REVIEW QUESTIONS

1. Why does the poet ask the woodman to spare the tree? 2. What kind of boy was Daffydowndilly? How did he like school? What did he see on his day out? Who was with him? 3. What had the boy Casabianca been told to do? How did he obey? 4. Who wrote "Home, Sweet Home"? Recite it. 5. Who wrote *Alice's Adventures in Wonderland?*

A LIST OF SYNONYMS

KEY TO PRONUNCIATIONS, AS GIVEN IN THE TEXT

The diacritical marks employed are those used in Webster's New International Dictionary.

An unmarked vowel is a slighted short vowel, usually unaccented.

ā as in fate	ĕ as in met	ō as in hole	ū as in pure
ă as in fat	ē as in her	ŏ as in hot	ŭ as in but
â as in fare	ī as in bite	ô as in lost	u̦ as in pull
ä as in father	ĭ as in bit	or, as in fall	ȳ as in my
ē as in me	ɳ as in bank	oo as in room	y̆ as in story

abound: to be plentiful (p. 49)
abused: ill-treated (p. 102)
abyss: a chasm (p. 302)
accompany: to go with (p. 67)
accumulate: to amass (p. 189)
accustomed: customary (p. 260)
agitated: excited, perturbed (p. 264)
agony: suffering, distress (p. 39)
alight: to get down (p. 59)
alter: to change (p. 97).
amazement: astonishment (p. 219)
ambitious: seeking honor (p. 189)
anchored: held fast (p. 57)
ancient: very old, antique (p. 25)
anguish: distress, sorrow (p. 302)
antics: pranks, tricks (p. 254)
approach: to come near to (p. 39)
appropriateness: suitability (p. 279)
approval: liking (p. 331)
approve: to like (p. 159)
assistance: help (p. 49)
assurance: confidence (p. 67)
attendance: presence (p. 189)
augment: to increase (p. 302)
aureole: a halo (p. 284)
autumn: fall (p. 284)
avowal: confession (p. 302)
awful: terrible (p. 159)

banish: to drive out (p. 151)
banter: to tease, to joke (p. 69)
bazaar: an Oriental shop (p. 57)
beach: shore, coast (p. 109)
beckon: to summon (p. 211)
beguile: to charm away (p. 336)

benevolent: kindly (p. 189)
bestir: to move about (p. 147)
bevies: flocks (p. 63)
bewildered: confused, dazed (p. 312)
bicker: to quarrel (p. 142)
billowy: wavy (p. 33)
blithe: gay, merry (p. 192)
blithesome: gay, cheerful (p. 111)
blockhouse: a fort (p. 178)
bramble: briar (p. 131)
brawny: muscular, strong (p. 268)
brimming: brimful (p. 142)
broidered: decorated (p. 151)
bustle: commotion (p. 63)
busy: occupied (p. 136)

calm: quiet, peaceful (p. 33)
caress: to fondle (p. 136)
cargo: freight (p. 170)
chagrin: annoyance (p. 189)
circumstances: conditions (p. 159)
civil: polite, well-bred (p. 348)
civility: politeness, courtesy (p. 44)
clumsy: awkward, gawky (p. 102)
commend: to praise (p. 39)
commodities: goods (p. 39)
commotion: excitement, turmoil (p. 74)
compassion: pity, sympathy (p. 211)
compounded: mixed, concocted (p. 292)
comrade: companion (p. 109)
concussion: a shock (p. 302)
conflict: a fight, combat, contest (p. 211)
confused: not clear, mixed (p. 19)
conjecture: guess, estimate (p. 297)

conquered: defeated, vanquished (p. 161)
conscientious: faithful, dutiful (p. 279)
considerable: a good deal (p. 49)
continuous: extending on (p. 105).
convey: to carry, transport (p. 25)
corporeal: bodily, physical (p. 189)
countenance: face, expression (p. 79)
craft: skill (p. 211)
crag: steep rock (p. 170)
creaking: squeaking (p. 74)
croft: small farm (p. 198)
crouch: to kneel (p. 170)

dank: damp (p. 198)
decrepit: weak, feeble (p. 49)
delectable: delicious, enjoyable (p. 292)
delicate: fine, dainty (p. 248)
deliverance: rescue, safety (p. 44)
depressed: sad, downhearted, discouraged (p. 102)
descend: to go or come down (p. 39)
desert: to forsake, to leave (p. 102)
designed: planned, intended (p. 39)
desolate: sad, lonesome (p. 151)
desperate: hopeless (p. 226)
desperation: despair, last hope (p. 302)
device: design, plan (p. 44)
devour: to eat greedily (p. 57)
discern: to see, to make out (p. 39)
disdain: haughtiness (p. 312)
disgrace: shame, discredit (p. 92)
dishevelled: disordered (p. 211)
dismay: fright, consternation (p. 325)
distend: to stretch (p. 284)
distinguish: to perceive (p. 39)
distinguished: famous (p. 97)
dodge: to avoid (p. 83)
doff: to take off (p. 192)
doubtless: certainly (p. 92)
drone: idler, lazy fellow (p. 147)
dwindle: to diminish (p. 198)

eager: keen, earnest (p. 178)
elastic: springy (p. 279)
embark: to go aboard (p. 292)
enchanted: magical (p. 292)
encounter: a struggle (p. 211)
ensign: standard, flag (p. 161)
entreat: beg, beseech (p. 159)
entry: arrival (p. 184)

equipage: horses and carriage (p. 189)
eschew: to reject, disregard (p. 124)
escort: to go with, attend (p. 226)
especially: particularly (p. 79)
estimable: good, worthy (p. 292)
estimate: a judgment (p. 189)
excellent: very fine (p. 49)
excessively: very much, too much (p. 90)
exclude: to shut out, reject (p. 44)
exhausted: tired out (p. 19)
exhilarate: to cheer, enliven (p. 49)
expedition: trip, journey (p. 292)
explore: look over, investigate (p. 49)
extremity: end (p. 297)

fabulous: fanciful (p. 44)
fanciful: imaginary (p. 97)
fastened: secured (p. 19)
fatigue: weariness (p. 49)
feasible: possible (p. 279)
fervently: earnestly (p. 159)
festival: celebration (p. 57)
fitful: occasional (p. 109)
flare: to gleam (p. 211)
flimsy: weak, frail (p. 302)
fondled: caressed (p. 204)
forgiven: pardoned (p. 138)
fragrant: sweet-smelling (p. 131)
frantically: wildly, excitedly (p. 264)
frightfully: terribly, fearfully (p. 90)
frolic: play (p. 147)
fulfilled: satisfied (p. 264)
furiously: wildly, savagely (p. 109)

generous: liberal, kind (p. 151)
gibbet: gallows (p. 279)
gigantic: huge (p. 292)
gnarled: rough (p. 131)
gratitude: thankfulness (p. 248)
guard: escort, watch (p. 25)

haggard: thin, wasted (p. 211)
hale: healthy, hearty (p. 192)
hallow: to make sacred, consecrate (p. 336)
haunts: resorts (p. 142)
haversack: knapsack (p. 248)
height: altitude, elevation (p. 39)
helm: steering-wheel (p. 170)
heritage: birthright, inheritance (p. 12)
hesitate: to pause (p. 325)
hospitality: kindness to a guest (p. 19)

illusion: deception (p. 302)
imaginable: conceivable (p. 79)
immediately: at once (p. 226)
impartially: equally, fairly (p. 151)
incessantly: uninterruptedly (p. 302)
inclination: wish, desire (p. 44)
incredible: unbelievable (p. 159)
indignant: angry (p. 102)
indulge: to favor (p. 219)
infirm: weak, feeble (p. 49)
ingenious: clever, gifted (p. 97)
innocent: guiltless, harmless (p. 284)
instance: example (p. 69)
instruct: to teach (p. 219)
interfere: to bother, obstruct (p. 84)
interrupt: to stop, halt (p. 307)
invigorate: to strengthen (p. 292)
invisible: unseen (p. 211)
irksome: tedious, tiresome (p. 307)

jagged: rough, sharp (p. 260)
jaunty: gay, jolly (p. 124)
jewels: gems, precious stones (p. 44)
jocund: gay, jolly (p. 105)
judgment: decision, opinion (p. 151)
jungle: a thick forest (p. 57)
justification: excuse (p. 159)

laudable: praiseworthy (p. 189)
laurel: emblem of victory (p. 151)
lea: meadow, open field (p. 69)
levee: social gathering (p. 189)
luggage: baggage (p. 159)
luminous: clear, bright (p. 307)

malignant: evil, hating (p. 302)
maniac: insane person (p. 307)
margin: edge, border (p. 63)
mariners: sailors, seamen (p. 39)
matronly: motherly (p. 74)
mead: meadow (p. 147)
meagre: small, slight, thin (p. 248)
meditate: to think, reflect (p. 297)
melancholy: sad, sober (p. 79)
men-of-war: war-ships (p. 25)
mercy: kindness, compassion (p. 19)
metropolis: principal city (p. 25)
mightily: powerfully, strongly (p. 97)
minaret: a slender spire (p. 57)
miraculous: wonderful (p. 39)
moderate: to keep down (p. 44)

moil: toil, hard work (p. 124)
momentary: very brief (p. 302)
monarch: king, emperor (p. 124)
monstrous: huge and horrible (p. 39)
moor: to tie fast (p. 292)
mosque: temple (p. 57)
mournfully: sadly (p. 84)
multitude: crowd, throng (p. 312)

narrate: to tell, relate (p. 44)
naughty: bad, mischievous (p. 102)
neglect: carelessness (p. 159)
negligence: carelessness (p. 159)
nestlings: young birds (p. 69)
nice: dainty, particular (p. 74)
nimble: active (p. 279)

obliged: compelled (p. 49)
occasionally: now and then (p. 219)
occupy: fill, hold (p. 92)
odorous: strong smelling (p. 219)
offend: to insult (p. 74)
omnipresent: everywhere (p. 307)
opportunities: chances (p. 284)
optical: visual (p. 302)

palate: taste (p. 49)
pallor: paleness (p. 307)
palpitate: to tremble (p. 211)
particular: careful (p. 184)
pensive: thoughtful, sad (p. 105)
perilous: dangerous (p. 307)
perplexity: doubt, difficulty (p. 39)
placid: quiet, peaceful, still (p. 219)
plumage: feathers (p. 211)
pomp: splendor (p. 124)
portrait: likeness, picture (p. 170)
pounce: to spring upon (p. 44)
precious: dear (p. 159)
precipice: steep rock (p. 44)
previous: former (p. 292)
prodigious: wonderful (p. 39)
profound: deep (p. 25)
promenade: walk (p. 285)
prone: flat (p. 219)
provisions: food (p. 39)

quantity: amount (p. 49)
quarrel: dispute (p. 92)

range: to wander freely (p. 33)
rapidity: speed (p. 39)

rapture: wild joy (p. 285)
recede: to go back (p. 297)
recognize: to know again, remember (p. 264)
recollection: memory (p. 90)
reel: to spin round (p. 211)
refresh: to strengthen (p. 184)
regal: kingly, royal (p. 124)
region: realm, place (p. 33)
registered: noted (p. 159)
rehearsed: practised (p. 219)
remarkable: unusual, notable (p. 226)
renown: fame, honor (p. 211)
repentance: remorse, regret (p. 39)
repose: rest (p. 268)
reprieve: pardon (p. 159)
reproach: to blame, scold (p. 226)
rescue: to save (p. 170)
resigned: submitted (p. 39)
resisted: objected, opposed (p. 90)
retinue: followers, escort (p. 25)
reward: pay, compensation (p. 84)
rugged: rough (p. 170)

sacrifice: to offer up (p. 189)
saluted: greeted, spoke to (p. 49)
savory: fragrant (p. 292)
score: twenty (p. 25)
scowl: frown (p. 219)
scruples: right principles (p. 279)
scud: to race, hurry (p. 109)
seaboard: seacoast (p. 292)
sensation: feeling (p. 189)
sentry: guard (p. 159)
sever: to separate, cut off (p. 151)
severity: sternness (p. 348)
sheen: gleam, brightness (p. 63)
sheer: straight (p. 254)
shingly: gravelly (p. 142)
significant: important (p. 292)
silence: quiet (p. 33)
sinewy: wiry, tough (p. 268)
solace: comfort, consolation (p. 336)
solitude: loneliness (p. 105)
spectator: onlooker (p. 312)
sphere: a globe, a place (p. 92)
sprightly: gay, lively (p. 105)
spry: active, quick, alert (p. 92)
spurn: scorn (p. 279)
stanch: firm, strong (p. 109)
stern: rear (p. 292)

stifle: to choke, smother (p. 285)
stokers: firemen (p. 170)
straightforward: honest (p. 159)
strain: a song (p. 147)
substantial: solid (p. 90)
sufficed: satisfied (p. 39)
sullen: cross, frowning (p. 109)
summon: to call (p. 226)
swamp: to sink, submerge (p. 170)
sward: turf (p. 124)

talents: abilities (p. 92)
terrified: frightened, alarmed (p. 74)
terror: fear, fright (p. 178)
thorpe: village (p. 142)
threatened: warned (p. 74)
torrents: floods (p. 170)
tractable: obedient, docile (p. 248)
transport: to carry, convey (p. 292)
treacherous: false, traitorous (p. 124)
tremendous: very great, terrible (p. 102)
tremor: fright, fear, terror (p. 226)
triumph: victory (p. 211)
tumult: confusion (p. 307)

upbraid: to reproach, blame (p. 39)
undaunted: unafraid, brave (p. 211)
urchins: small boys (p. 74)

vacancy: emptiness (p. 302)
vacant: empty, idle (p. 105)
valiant: brave, courageous (p. 102)
vanish: to disappear (p. 254)
vanquished: defeated (p. 161)
vehicle: wagon, or car (p. 25)
venture: to dare, to risk (p. 90)
vexation: annoyance (p. 189)
victual: food (p. 219)
vigorously: strongly (p. 248)
violent: fierce, rough (p. 19)
vivid: bright, brilliant (p. 279)
voluntarily: willingly (p. 189)
volunteer: to offer (p. 297)
voyage: a trip at sea (p. 39)

wanes: passes (p. 147)
wealth: riches (p. 33)
wrench: to twist (p. 19)
wroth: angry (p. 109)
wry: crooked (p. 279)

Printed in the United States of America.

Lightning Source UK Ltd.
Milton Keynes UK
UKOW011837270912

199758UK00006B/35/P